# BARFORD REMEMBERS

WWI and WWII
The Men Who Fought and The Families They Left Behind

BARFORD HERITAGE GROUP

First published in 2015 by

Barford Heritage Group

www.barfordheritage.org



ISBN: 978-0-9565248-1-2

Printed by Warwick Printing Company Limited

## CONTENTS

We used to search for bird's nests

In the wild hedgerow,

And sit and make long daisy chains,

All those years ago.

Like a floral carpet,

The meadow, full of flowers,

We remember sunny days,

Forgotten are the showers.

Perhaps the meadow is still there;

I haven't been to see.

I am happy to remember

The way it used to be.

Hazel Taylor A Barford villager

## Foreword

Why did Barford Heritage Group decide to compile this book? After all, a plethora of publications about the 1914-1918 conflict have been produced in this the centenary of the Great War. We were interested in researching the human stories behind the facts as they affected our rural Warwickshire village.

One hundred years on, the task of investigating the consequences to Barford of Foreign Secretary Edward Grey's sombre statement that "the lights are going out all over Europe" was daunting. No one is alive to tell the tale and many relevant public records, including photographs, have been destroyed by fire.

Would we be able to discover how the menfolk – young and not so young – felt about the imminent conflict?

What of the women called to step out of their traditional and often subservient roles?

What was the result of the sudden influx of strangers into the community in the form of evacuees, billeted soldiers and the girls of the Women's Land Army?

How did the children fare?

Were horses from Barford commandeered? After all, we know there were vast marshalling centres at nearby Warwick and Kineton.

Were there food shortages as rationing of sugar, meat, butter, cheese and margarine had been introduced by April 1918?

The widows of the fallen and wives of those injured were not automatically granted a pension. This resulted in some suffering extreme poverty. Was this the experience of any dependants in Barford?

Questions, questions!

At the start of the war, Britain thought herself to be invincible. Encouraged or shamed into volunteering by their womenfolk, exhorted from the pulpit and praised by their elders, young men, often with their friends and workmates, queued to enlist with patriotic fervour in the belief that 'it would all be over by Christmas'. They set forth with confidence only to face unimaginable carnage in the 'meat-grinder' of trench warfare.

We know the names of the fallen and in most cases where they lived in Barford. We know their fate and where they lie. It has rightly been said that we had a new vision of youth in those days. The world turned to young men as the saviours of liberty. As for the rest, entrenched attitudes were forced to change and far-reaching reforms in social life were set in train. Life for most inhabitants could certainly never be the same again.

So, the following chapters try to create a tapestry woven from local newspaper accounts and diverse archive sources, supported throughout by the reminiscences of villagers who were but children at the time.

What was life like a hundred years ago for the six to seven hundred inhabitants of Barford as they lived year after year at an unhurried pace?

A few wealthy paternalistic members of society organised matters of health, education and welfare for the less fortunate. The district nurse and midwife was financed by subscriptions and donations. Craftsmen and artisans abounded, blacksmiths and wheelwrights prospered.

The Gas Works on the Wellesbourne Road provided fuel for cooking and street lighting. Every house would have needed a fence and a gate for this was a time before cattle trucks. Sheep or cattle on their way to markets in Warwick or Stratford would fill a street, herded by a drover and his dog.

The gentle pattern of life was punctuated by entertainment and merry-making. In Barford, the Friendly Societies, the Foresters and the Oddfellows continued to be supported after the 1911 National Insurance Act. Their 'Club Days', when feasting and dancing followed a banner-led procession accompanied by the Barford Drum and Fife Band, was an annual highlight. Similarly May Day, with school children performing intricate ribbon-dances around a maypole, flower shows, sports, drama, Boy Scouts and church festivals involved the entire population. Many of these activities took place in the Ryland Hall, built for community use by Mrs E Smith-Ryland, located behind the arts and crafts house modestly named 'The Cottage' in Church Street. So for many residents there was little incentive to venture far outside the village and their placid lives continued.

Barford, Church Street

# Introduction

## Life in Barford at the start of WWI

The most comprehensive insight into Barford before WWI is given by the results of the 1911 census. This data has limitations. For instance although households are grouped by street, they are not given in order and it is difficult in many cases to be sure exactly where families lived. And of course it is only a snapshot on a particular day, when some residents would have been away and others were included as visitors. However, the information gives a valuable insight into age profiles, occupations and the mobility of families at that time and some further guidance has been obtained from current residents of Barford whose families go back to this time.

The total population in the village in 1911 was six hundred and forty-three. This number includes all those in Bridge Street, Wellesbourne Road, Church Street, Keytes Lane, High Street and Barford Hill, but it excludes the outlying houses and farms – Plestowes, Gooseberry Farm, Hareway Farm and Westham House.

The mobility of families and individuals at the time was higher than might be expected. Of the total population, 35% had been born in Barford, 29% elsewhere in Warwickshire and 35% elsewhere in the UK. Six people had been born overseas (two in India, one in Australia, one in Germany and two in France). While not cosmopolitan, this does suggest a village with plentiful contacts and influences from the outside world.

The distribution of the population by age group in Barford at this time is shown in Chart 1. At first sight this appears fairly normal, but the groupings disguise a couple of unexpected results.

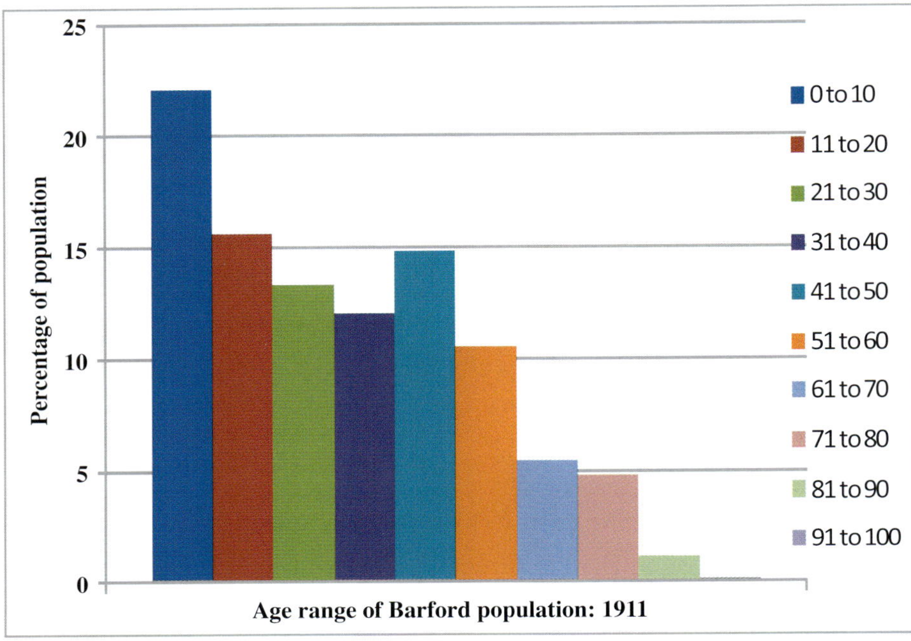


Chart 1: Age distribution of Barford residents – 1911

In this age distribution chart, contained within the 22% of the total population in the 0 to 10 year group (blue bar) 13% were aged 5 or under. This suggests either a recent surge in birth rate, or a high mortality rate in this age group. In the 11 to 20 age group (red bar) 6% are aged 16 to 20 years. A higher rate of leaving the village in the age group 21 to 30 is reflected in the lower than expected percentage of 5% of 16 to 20 year olds remaining in the village.

The youngest person in the village was an as yet unnamed baby boy less than a month old, born to Herbert and Sarah Lines of Westham Cottage. The oldest resident was Martha Clarke, a 92 year old widow living by herself in Bridge Street.

Just less than 50% of the village population was described in the census as having an occupation.

Those in domestic service dominated the number in work, being 31% in total, some being listed in their place of employment and some within their own families. Between them, domestic servants, farmers and farm workers and domestic gardeners represent nearly 60% of the work force. Farm workers as a group include various specialties such as stockmen, dairy workers, shepherds, poultrymen and ploughboys; even a steam plough engineer is included under this heading. Craftsmen include a dozen different occupations ranging from blacksmiths, carpenters and wheelwrights to needlewomen, haberdashers and dressmakers.

| Occupation group | Proportion |
|---|---|
| **Domestic servants** | **31.0%** |
| **Farmers and farm workers** | **15.6%** |
| **Domestic gardeners** | **12.7%** |
| **Craftsmen** | **11.3%** |
| **Builders and labourers** | **8.7%** |
| **Retailers** | **7.7%** |
| **Professional and clerical** | **4.6%** |
| **Miscellaneous** | **4.0%** |
| **Private means** | **3.7%** |
| **Military** | **0.7%** |

**Distribution of occupations in Barford at 1911**

A better insight into the village at this time is given by a brief review of who was living where and what they were doing. This is shown street by street in the following sections.

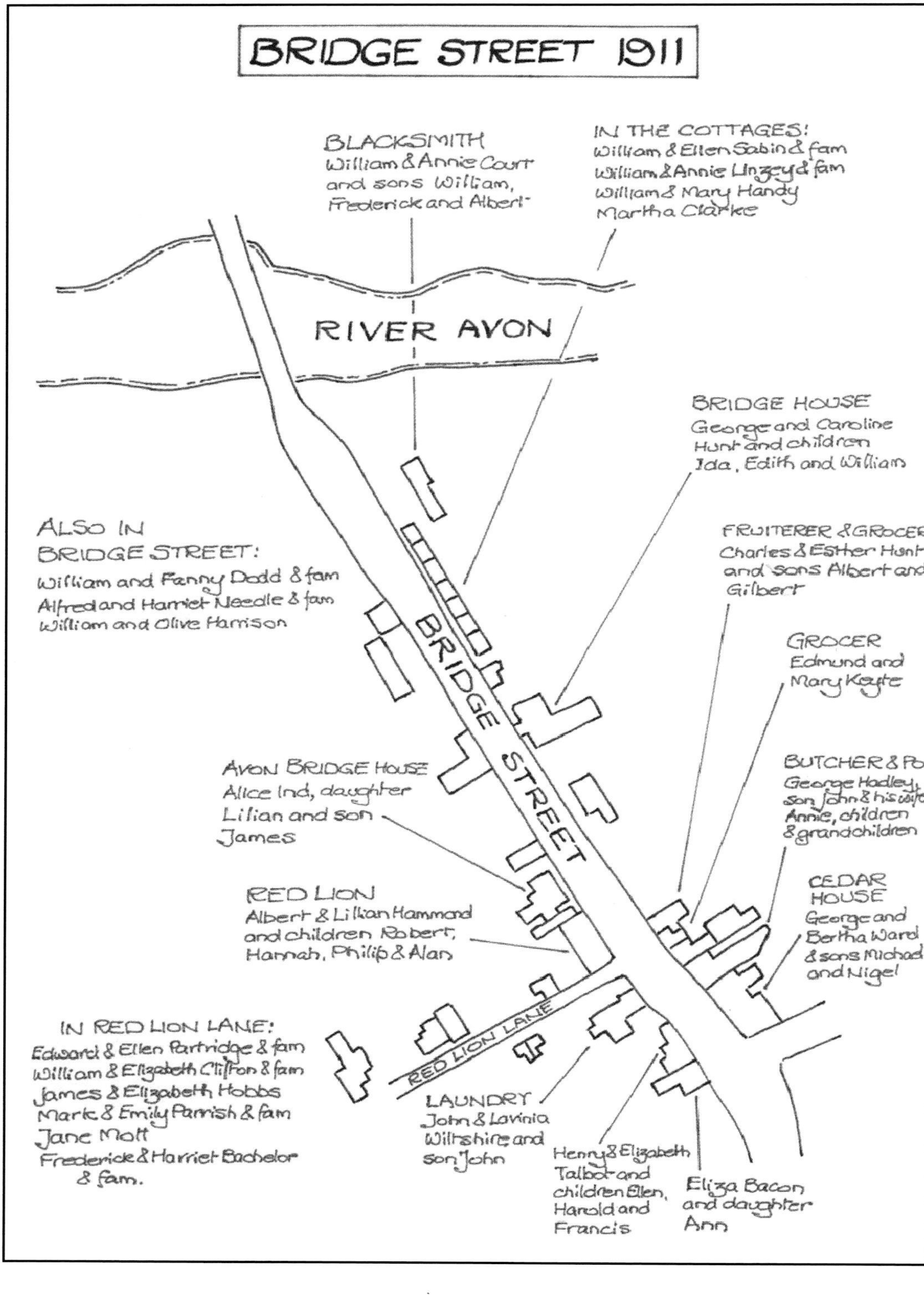
BRIDGE STREET 1911
BLACKSMITH
William & Annie Court
and sons William,
Frederick and Albert
IN THE COTTAGES:
William & Ellen Sabin & fam
William & Annie Linzey & fam
William & Mary Handy
Martha Clarke
RIVER AVON
BRIDGE HOUSE
George and Caroline
Hunt and children
Ida, Edith and William
ALSO IN
BRIDGE STREET:
William and Fanny Dodd & fam
Alfred and Harriet Needle & fam
William and Olive Harrison
FRUITERER & GROCER
Charles & Esther Hunt
and sons Albert and
Gilbert
BRIDGE STREET
GROCER
Edmund and
Mary Keyte
AVON BRIDGE HOUSE
Alice Ind, daughter
Lilian and son
James
BUTCHER & Po
George Hadley,
son John & his wife
Annie, children
& grandchildren
CEDAR
HOUSE
George and
Bertha Ward
& sons Michael
and Nigel
RED LION
Albert & Lilian Hammond
and children Robert,
Hannah, Philip & Alan
IN RED LION LANE:
Edward & Ellen Partridge & fam
William & Elizabeth Clifton & fam
James & Elizabeth Hobbs
Mark & Emily Parrish & fam
Jane Mott
Frederick & Harriet Bachelor
& fam.
RED LION LANE
LAUNDRY
John & Lavinia
Wiltshire and
son John
Henry & Elizabeth
Talbot and
children Ellen,
Harold and
Francis
Eliza Bacon
and daughter
Ann

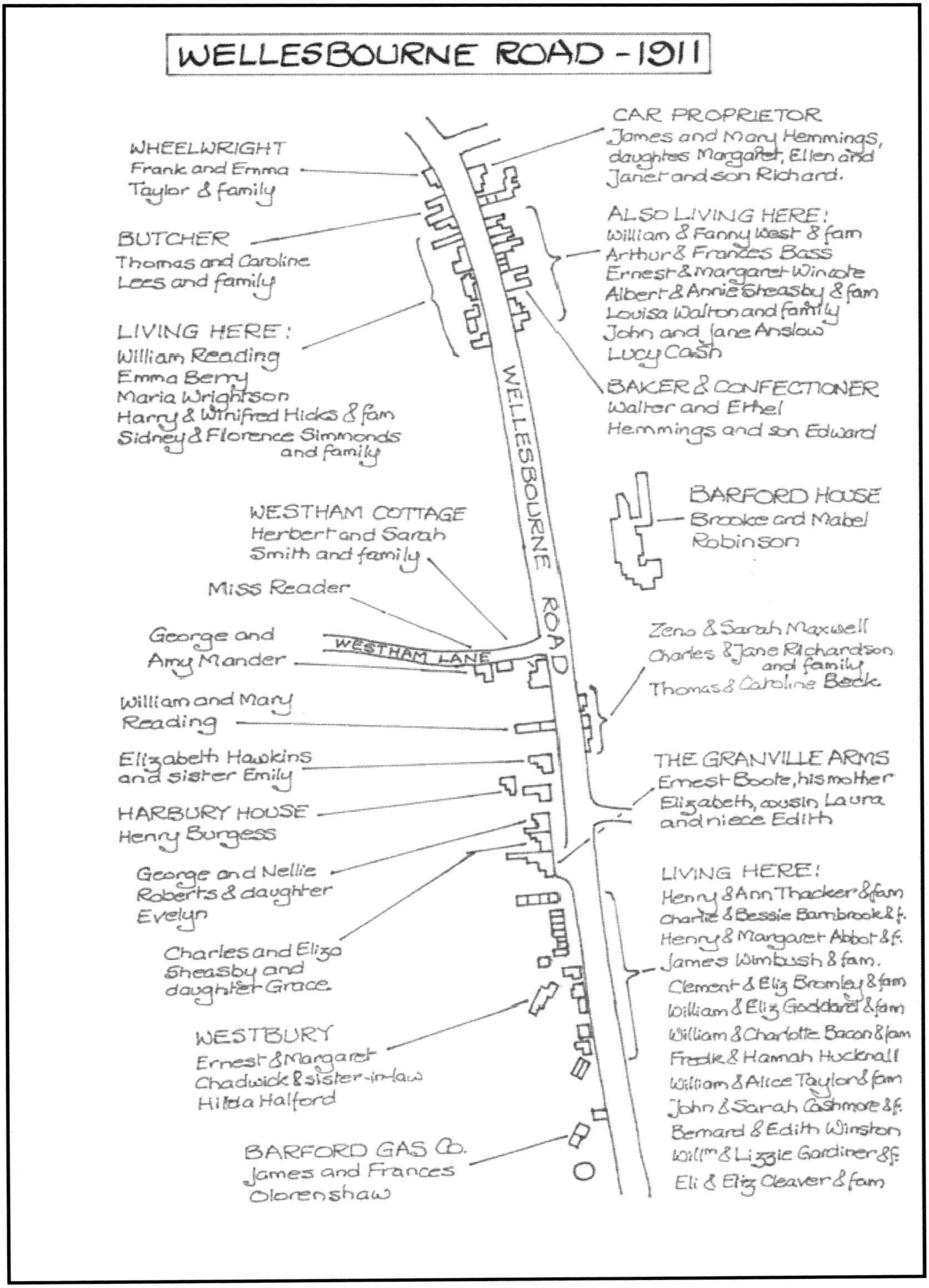
WELLESBOURNE ROAD - 1911
CAR PROPRIETOR
James and Mary Hemmings, daughters Margaret, Ellen and Janet and son Richard.
WHEELWRIGHT
Frank and Emma Taylor & family
BUTCHER
Thomas and Caroline Lees and family
ALSO LIVING HERE:
William & Fanny West & fam
Arthur & Frances Bass
Ernest & Margaret Wincote
Albert & Annie Sheasby & fam
Louisa Walton and family
John and Jane Anslow
Lucy Cash
LIVING HERE:
William Reading
Emma Berry
Maria Wrightson
Harry & Winifred Hicks & fam
Sidney & Florence Simmonds and family
BAKER & CONFECTIONER
Walter and Ethel Hemmings and son Edward
WELLESBOURNE ROAD
BARFORD HOUSE
Brooke and Mabel Robinson
WESTHAM COTTAGE
Herbert and Sarah Smith and family
Miss Reader
George and Amy Mander
WESTHAM LANE
Zeno & Sarah Maxwell
Charles & Jane Richardson and family
Thomas & Caroline Beck
William and Mary Reading
Elizabeth Hawkins and sister Emily
THE GRANVILLE ARMS
Ernest Boote, his mother Elizabeth, cousin Laura and niece Edith
HARBURY HOUSE
Henry Burgess
George and Nellie Roberts & daughter Evelyn
LIVING HERE:
Henry & Ann Thacker & fam
Charlie & Bessie Bambrook & f.
Henry & Margaret Abbot & f.
James Wimbush & fam.
Clement & Eliz Bromley & fam
William & Eliz Goddard & fam
William & Charlotte Bacon & fam
Freddie & Hannah Hucknall
William & Alice Taylor & fam
John & Sarah Cashmore & f.
Bernard & Edith Winston
Willm & Lizzie Gardiner & f.
Eli & Eliz Cleaver & fam
Charles and Eliza Sheasby and daughter Grace.
WESTBURY
Ernest & Margaret Chadwick & sister-in-law Hilda Halford
BARFORD GAS Co.
James and Frances Olorenshaw

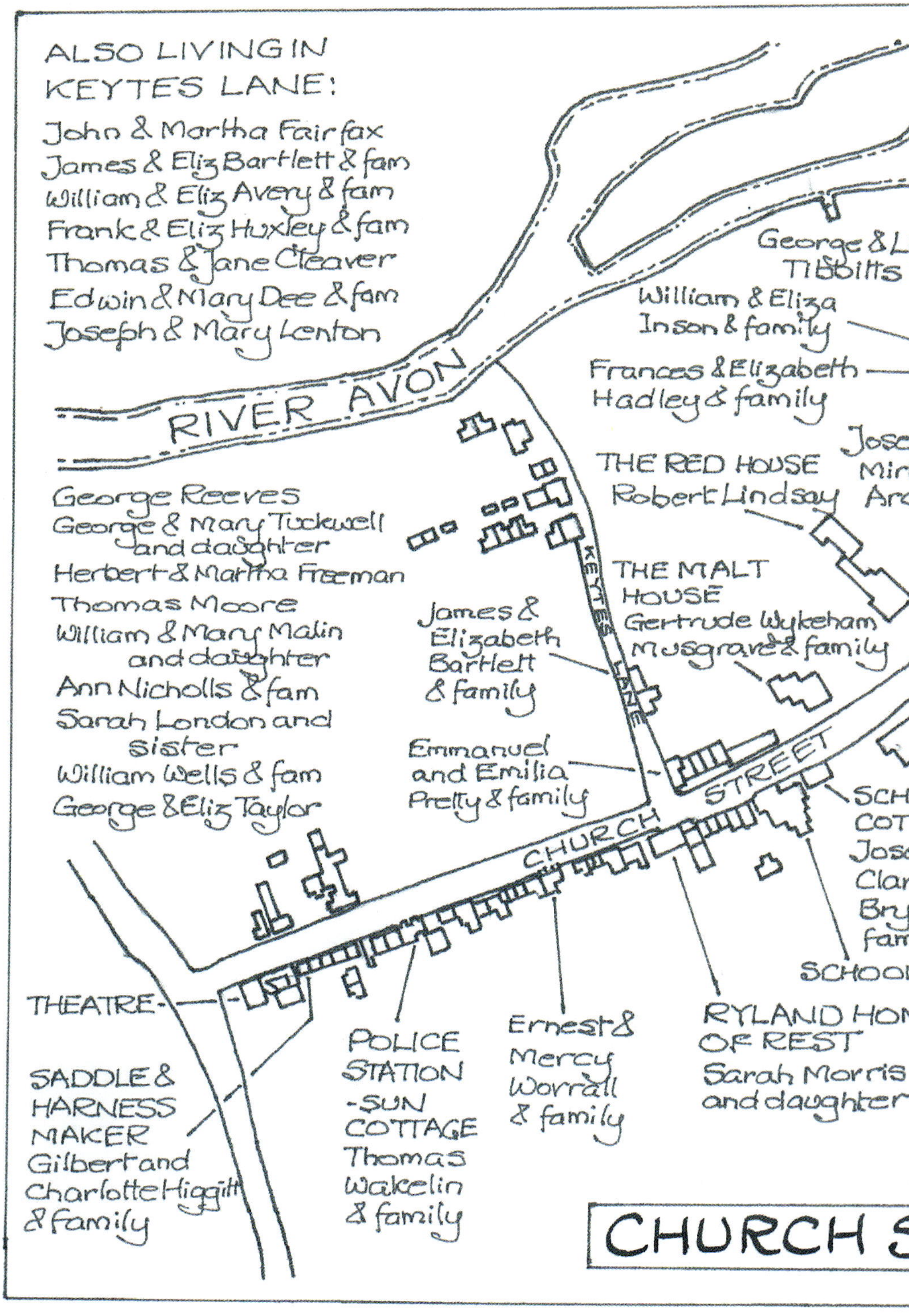
ALSO LIVING IN KEYTES LANE:
John & Martha Fairfax
James & Eliz Bartlett & fam
William & Eliz Avery & fam
Frank & Eliz Huxley & fam
Thomas & Jane Cleaver
Edwin & Mary Dee & fam
Joseph & Mary Lenton
RIVER AVON
William & Eliza Inson & family
Frances & Elizabeth Hadley & family
THE RED HOUSE Robert Lindsay
George Reeves
George & Mary Tuckwell and daughter
Herbert & Martha Freeman
Thomas Moore
William & Mary Malin and daughter
Ann Nicholls & fam
Sarah London and sister
William Wells & fam
George & Eliz Taylor
KEYTES LANE
THE MALT HOUSE Gertrude Wykeham Musgrave & family
James & Elizabeth Bartlett & family
Emmanuel and Emilia Pretty & family
CHURCH STREET
SCHOOL
THEATRE
SADDLE & HARNESS MAKER Gilbert and Charlotte Higgitt & family
POLICE STATION - SUN COTTAGE Thomas Wakelin & family
Ernest & Mercy Worrall & family
RYLAND HOME OF REST Sarah Morris and daughter

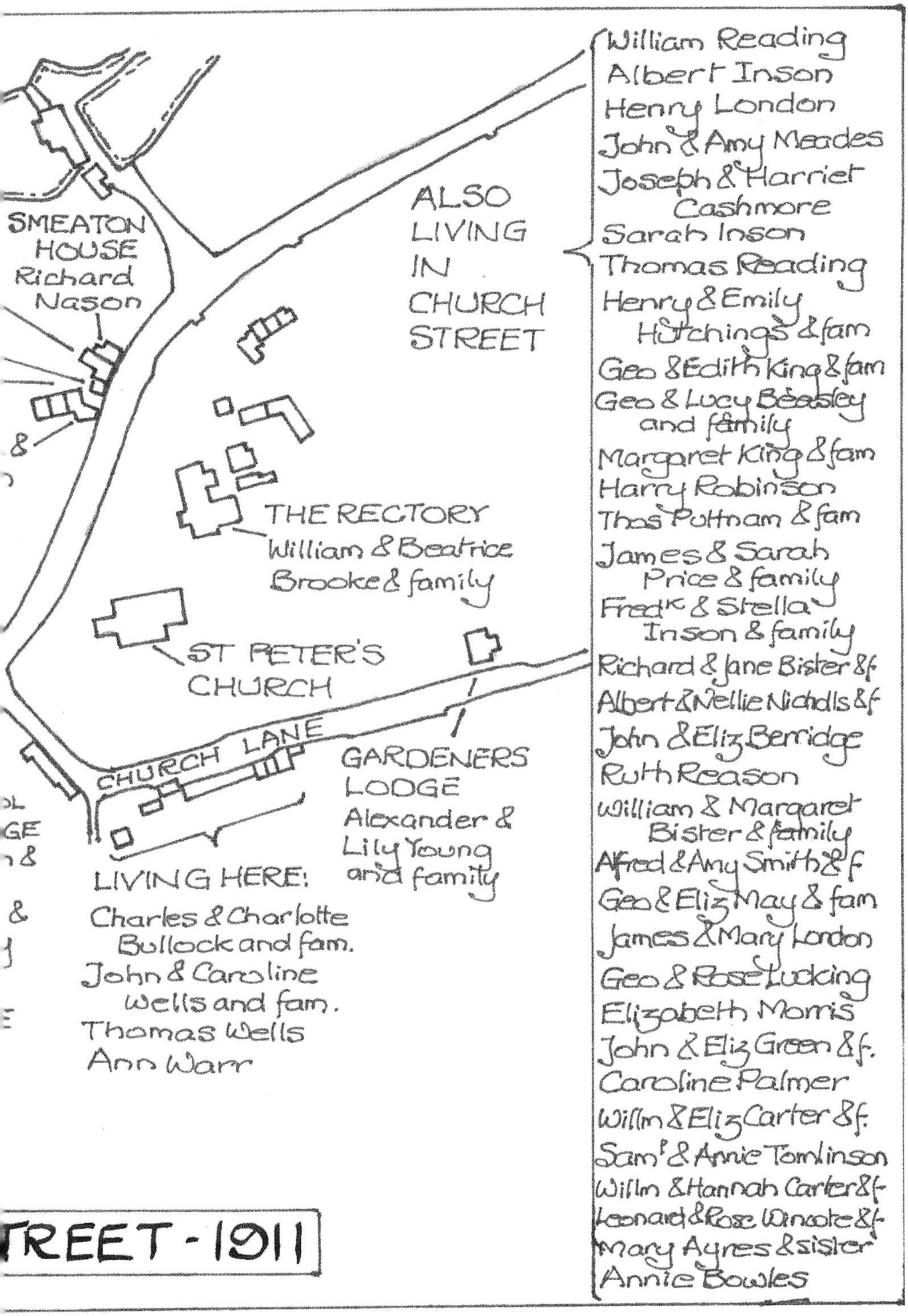
SMEATON HOUSE
Richard Nason
THE RECTORY
William & Beatrice Brooke & family
ST PETER'S CHURCH
CHURCH LANE
GARDENERS LODGE
Alexander & Lily Young and family
LIVING HERE:
Charles & Charlotte Bullock and fam.
John & Caroline Wells and fam.
Thomas Wells
Ann Warr
ALSO LIVING IN CHURCH STREET
William Reading
Albert Inson
Henry London
John & Amy Meades
Joseph & Harriet Cashmore
Sarah Inson
Thomas Reading
Henry & Emily Hutchings & fam
Geo & Edith King & fam
Geo & Lucy Beasley and family
Margaret King & fam
Harry Robinson
Thos Puttnam & fam
James & Sarah Price & family
Fredk & Stella Inson & family
Richard & Jane Bister & f.
Albert & Nellie Nicholls & f.
John & Eliz Berridge
Ruth Reason
William & Margaret Bister & family
Alfred & Amy Smith & f
Geo & Eliz May & fam
James & Mary London
Geo & Rose Lucking
Elizabeth Morris
John & Eliz Green & f.
Caroline Palmer
Willm & Eliz Carter & f.
Saml & Annie Tomlinson
Willm & Hannah Carter & f.
Leonard & Rose Wincote & f.
Mary Ayres & sister
Annie Bowles
TREET - 1911

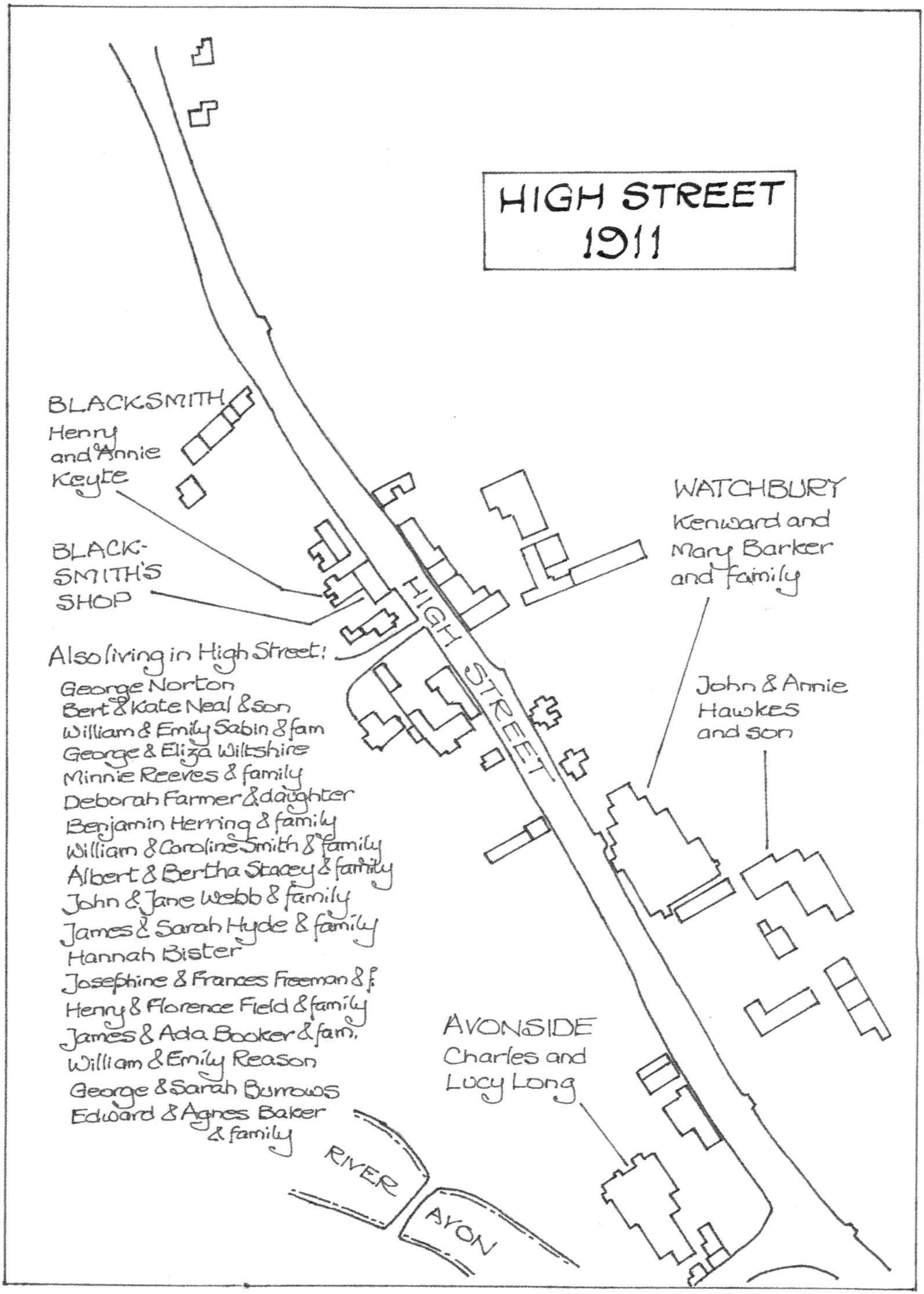
HIGH STREET
1911
BLACKSMITH
Henry
and Annie
Keyte
BLACK-
SMITH'S
SHOP
Also living in High Street:
George Norton
Bert & Kate Neal & son
William & Emily Sabin & fam
George & Eliza Wiltshire
Minnie Reeves & family
Deborah Farmer & daughter
Benjamin Herring & family
William & Caroline Smith & family
Albert & Bertha Stacey & family
John & Jane Webb & family
James & Sarah Hyde & family
Hannah Bister
Josephine & Frances Freeman & f.
Henry & Florence Field & family
James & Ada Booker & fam.
William & Emily Reason
George & Sarah Burrows
Edward & Agnes Baker
& family
WATCHBURY
Kenward and
Mary Barker
and family
John & Annie
Hawkes
and son
HIGH
STREET
AVONSIDE
Charles and
Lucy Long
RIVER
AVON

## Barford in 1913

The grounds of Barford House were the venue for a Pageant of English history in seven episodes written by the schoolmaster, Mr W H Turner, and performed on 31st July 1913. Most of the costumes were made by the school children under the direction of Miss Hillson. The purpose of the Pageant was to raise funds for uniforms for the Barford Scout Troop.

Parts were played by F Baker, Godfrey Turner, William Hunt, B Hammond, Sidney Barnbrook, J Court, Seymour Bromley, B Wincote, Iris Baker, Cecil Wimbush, Jack Court, Nancy Hammond, May Gardiner and Tom Inson. John Bennett and the Morris Men of Ilmington provided music and dancing in the second part of the performance. It was a really joyous occasion.

However, Mr Turner's time as Headmaster ended in early 1914; he was evicted, his possessions thrown on Church Street, in front of the schoolhouse, and the eviction supervised by the Vicar, William Ingham Brooke, who had so lately praised him. All this over an unpaid drapery bill for a dress for Mrs Turner.

**Life for everyone was soon to change forever.**

Almost one year after the Pageant, on 17th July 1914, the 20th annual show of the Barford, Sherbourne and Wasperton Horticultural Society took place in the grounds of Barford Hill House. The entries were numerous and the music of the Yeomanry Band added joy to the occasion. Major W Pepys, Committee Chairman, referred to the loss sustained in the village by the death of the squire, Mr C S Smith-Ryland. A wide range of produce was exhibited. Many of those who won prizes, or members of their families, enlisted in the following months. On 28th July 1914 the Austro-Hungarians had declared war on Serbia, Germany invaded Belgium and Luxembourg and was moving towards France, leading Britain to declare war on Germany.

In the months before the start of the War, the Warwickshire Yeomanry carried out manoeuvres near Barford. On one occasion, forty men paraded in the village under the command of Captain Marchant, who lived in Hareway Lane. They had to construct a raft to transport a Maxim gun, baggage and saddlery across the river. At 10 pm that evening one of the sections was forced to retire back into the village. There were a large number of interested spectators. The Red Cross flag was flying from a temporary hospital of the Warwick Voluntary Aid Detachment (VAD) where every care was taken of the 'wounded'.

The proclamation to mobilise the armed forces was signed by the King at 11 am on 4th August 1914.

The Hunt family, who worked in Barford Post Office, were suddenly very busy receiving and sending out telegrams to reservists, informing them of their mobilisation and asking them to report to their regimental depots. There were only about a dozen telephones in the village at the time. Barford Post Office phone number was 'Barford 1'. The car proprietor on the Wellesbourne Road, J E Hemmings, was 'Barford 7' and he was busy transporting the called-up reservists.

The Warwickshire Territorial Force who had departed for their annual camp at Rhyl, on Bank Holiday Monday, 1st August, were recalled on the 2nd.

## Barford Rifle Club

Barford Rifle Club met twice weekly at the miniature Rifle Range on Bridge Street owned by the Smith-Ryland family. They held regular shooting matches against neighbouring villages.

Rifle Clubs had become popular after the Boer War, when the British suffered heavy losses as a result of the Boer's expert use of long-range rifles. Politicians such as Lord Salisbury encouraged their formation.

The earliest records of Barford Rifle Club detail a meeting held at the Red Lion pub (now the Joseph Arch) in October 1911. The meeting was chaired by the Rev Ingham Brooke, and attended by Messrs Chadwick, W Hawksworth, Hemming, A Hammond, Taylor, A Needle, R Jones, B Winston, G May and W Bacon. Together they elected a President Mr C A Smith-Ryland; Vice-President Rev Ingham Brooke; and Secretary A Hammond. B Winston was declared Captain, with James Harrison as his Vice, and J Chadwick as Treasurer. William Hawksworth was to be Rangewarden, for which he was paid £1 for the season. This can be measured against the cost of a .22 Lee Enfield Service Pattern rifle, which cost upwards of 85 shillings at that time (£4.25) and the cost of smokeless ammunition, which was 11s. 6d. per one thousand rounds.

The Range was also used by the Boy Scouts and the St John Ambulance for drill purposes, for which they were charged 2s. 6d. per night.

The meetings were well attended, and Barford regularly won their matches, beating Ashorne, Offchurch, Leamington, Tachbrook and Snitterfield. They won the South Warwickshire Challenge Cup in August 1913, and in February 1914 even won their match against 7 Battalion Royal Warwickshire regiment, winning by 51 points.

Inevitably the situation changed dramatically with the outbreak of war, as many of the members enlisted or were called away, and records become very sporadic.

No. 83

BARFORD RIFLE CLUB

| 1. | 2. | 3. | 4. | 5. | 6. | 7. | 8. | 9. |
|---|---|---|---|---|---|---|---|---|
| A. WINSTON | A. HAMMOND | ? | ? | R. JONES | ? | FRANK TAYLOR | ? | W. BACON |

| 10. | 11. | 12. | 13. | 14. | 15. | 16. |
|---|---|---|---|---|---|---|
| J. HYDE | ? | C. HUNT | B. WINSTON | ? | ? | L. HARRISON |

Instead of twice weekly matches, there are just two fixtures recorded during the rest of 1914, and one in 1915, from which time match records cease completely until 1919. A meeting of the Club was held in December 1914, at which the only resolution taken was that two Lee Enfield rifles, which at a previous pre-war meeting had been declared redundant and to be put up for sale, should be retained.

The new President elected, in 1914, was Mr H Dennis Smith-Ryland. There is a record of only one further meeting of the Rifle Club during the war, in September 1916, at which it was proposed that the Rifle Range be opened for instruction and rifle shooting during the winter months. The boys' subscription was set at one shilling, which could be paid by installments.

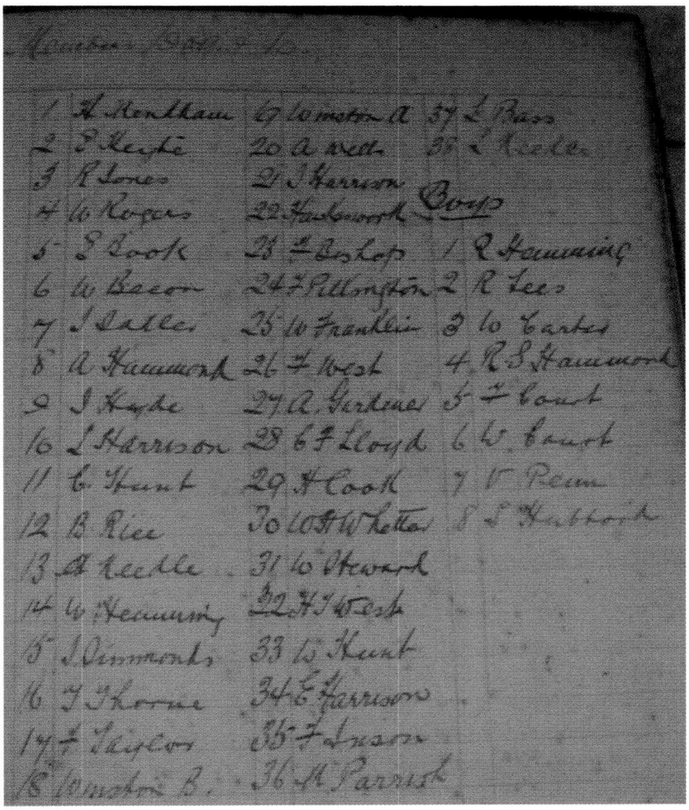

Following the sad loss of its Chairman, Captain H Dennis Smith-Ryland, and at least two of its active members, Albert Winston and Charles Wesley Hunt, there are no further records of the Rifle Club until 22nd May 1920, when it was proposed that the Club be reformed under the Presidency of Charles Ivor Smith-Ryland. Thereafter the Range was used frequently for dancing classes, whist drives and the Women's Institute.

## Changes to village life

A G Clifton, Red Lion Lane and H Wright, 9 High Street, enlisted in the Warwickshire Yeomanry in September 1914. R Dean enlisted in October 1914.

Colonel Long who lived at Avonside was assisting in buying horses for the army.

The grocery shops in Barford experienced a great increase in trade as customers bought stocks of sugar, tinned meat, tea and coffee. Flour was easily obtained as the Barford Flour Mill was still operating. Most people kept a pig and chickens and grew their own vegetables and there were a couple of big orchards in the village.

The wool and haberdashery shop in Church Street was a hive of activity as ladies purchased wool to knit comforts for the men.

Barford had a number of established clubs at this time. The Cricket Club had flourished in the village since 1851. As well as the summer match season they met for 'smoking' evenings in the Working Men's Club. There was also a football club. Tennis was played on the courts at the Red House and at Watchbury but there was no village tennis club at this time. Soon many of the members of these clubs would answer the call of the recruiting sergeants.

BARFORD FOOTBALL CLUB 1911/12. The people identified in this group are James Harrison in the front row holding the football, Walter (Bob) Hemmings, in the back row, far right, and in the second from back row, far left, William Bacon and next to him Thomas Chadwick. William Bacon was the Barford policeman and decorator. (Photograph: H.L. Young – WM)

During the War years the Reverend William Ingham Brooke (1863 – 1923) was Vicar of St Peter's Barford. He was a member of the Parish Council and played a very full part in village life. He and his wife, Beatrice, were supporters of the suffragette movement and invited some of the leaders to speak in Barford. He had five daughters, including Faith who went on to become an architect, unusual in 1915. His son Joshua Rupert Ingham Brooke was a captain in the Royal Garrison Artillery. Rev Ingham Brooke was chaplain to the forces from 1903 – 1905 and from 1917 – 1919. He had strong views on enlisting saying:

***We are very sorry still to see some young men about not in uniform. We can see by their faces they are ashamed of themselves and no wonder! Poor miserable creatures, they are missing the great opportunity of their lives. But it is not too late even now. Let them remember that they are fine men and let them avoid the conduct of the slave. They will be able to look their fellow citizens in the face when they have enlisted.***

The Roll of Honour of men who had enlisted was displayed outside the Post Office in Bridge Street for all to see.

White feathers were sent to eligible young men who did not answer the call to enlist.

**And so they enlisted.**

## More men needed

In November 1914 a large convoy of sixty-two motorcars arrived in Barford. In the cars were representatives of the Royal Warwickshire Regiment, Warwickshire Yeomanry, Warwickshire Horse Artillery, Army Service Corps, Army Veterinary Corps and staff from the Old Barracks in Warwick. When the cars halted, the men marched from the Wellesbourne Road along Church Street. Young Barford men came to see what it was all about. They were accosted by energetic recruiting sergeants who asked, "Won't you come and join us?" Literature was also distributed.

Major John Hall-Edwards, a Birmingham surgeon, who was the first to apply the new technology of X-rays to medical treatment in 1896, was in one of the cars. He was known as the X-ray martyr as he had sacrificed his arms in the cause of medical research.

People cheered as the long line of cars departed. News from the front soon began to reach the village. In July 1915 Private Andrews, Warwickshire Yeomanry, had been wounded. He was the son of Mr F A Andrews, house steward at Barford Hill House.

FIVE MEMBERS OF STAFF AT BARFORD HILL HOUSE about 1910. The directories include the names of F.A. Andrews, house steward; George Farmer, coachman; Richard Jones, gardener and William L. Maynard, engineer. Can these men be any of these? Another Barford Hill gardener, subsequently Drummer H.V. Penn, was awarded the Distinguished Service Medal for carrying messages under heavy fire in 1915 at the age of eighteen. He described the experience in a letter as being 'warmer than Barford Hill in the summer time'. (WM)

## School 1914 – 1918

When Barford St Peter's School reopened after the summer holidays on 31st August 1914 almost the full roll of one hundred pupils attended. During this winter attendance was low, due to an outbreak of whooping cough and influenza. There were no antibiotics then. Diseases such as mumps, measles and ringworm were common ailments at this time. The school medical officer called to check the children and to exclude pupils who were found to be ill.

In July 1914 a Barford groom, F C Heydon, was summoned for neglecting to have his child vaccinated. Mr Heydon said that his child was suffering from the effects of cutting his teeth and that he wished to have his own doctor perform the vaccination. The case was adjourned for one month and the defendant was ordered to pay 5s costs.

In November 1915 the name of a child suffering from tuberculosis was removed from the register and the child was deemed unlikely to return. In April 1917 the school was closed for a month because of scarlet fever. It was closed again in January 1918 due to whooping cough and deep snow. Influenza closed the school for a further week in July 1918.

A new sewing table was delivered to the school; sewing for the war effort was in full swing in the village and it was decided that the schoolgirls should learn.

The school inspector was a frequent visitor; in March 1915 he noted that 'this school has had to endure many vicissitudes of late'. He also noted that 'enunciation is clearer but still leaves a good deal to be desired'. The frequent colds would not be helping 'clear enunciation'!

Later in March 1915 the children were allowed to go to Wellesbourne Road to see the Surrey Yeomanry, who had been billeted in the village, depart for the front.

During the winter of 1915 and again in 1916 the school was closed for some days because of a shortage of coal and because of heavy snow. There was some really bad weather during these years. Many trees were uprooted.

With all the days missed due to illness and lack of coal it is not surprising that the school log book does not say how many children received prizes for good attendance from Miss N Smith-Ryland and Rev Ingham Brooke. Rose Elizabeth Avery aged 13, daughter of William Avery of Keytes Lane, received a silver watch in recognition of her attendance at school for eight years without missing one day.

Despite all these hardships the school pupils continued to pass their V1 Standard and scholarship exams.

There were occasional treats such as tea and games in the Rectory gardens in the summer. The school was closed for a half-day for the marriage of Miss Noel Smith-Ryland on 16th February 1916.

In 1915 Madge Ireland, the smallest scholar who attended the Wesleyan Sunday School, presented a bouquet to Mrs Bursnall of Leamington who visited the Wesleyan Methodist Church.

Most of the children were sent out picking blackberries in September 1917 to make jam for the army. They picked a total of 174lb! They were out picking again in September 1918 for the Government jam making scheme.

Daisy, Countess of Warwick, wrote to the newspapers about the problem of taking children out of school for this type of work. At this time she was friendly with Joseph Arch and often visited him in his cottage in Barford. It is likely that he influenced her to write this article stating that the only hope the poor had to escape from a life of hunger and drudgery was to obtain an education. At this time farm labourers were paid about 2s. 6d. a week and children about 1s. 6d. a day. The Countess of Warwick suggested that it would be better if the well-fed children from the public schools were sent out to work the land!

On 11th November 1918 the gun for Warwick Gun Week passed through the village. Reports of the signing of the German Armistice came through as the children were waiting to see the gun. The school closed for the rest of the day.

In December 1918 two captured German guns, on a tour through Warwickshire spent the night outside the school. The same night a concert was held in the Ryland Hall in which every child took part.

## Soldiers from the East Surrey Yeomanry billeted in Barford

With over a million men answering Kitchener's call for volunteers there were no barracks available to shelter them and so they were moved from town to village all over the country for training before they were sent to the front. During the winter of 1914-1915, fifteen thousand men were billeted in this way in Warwickshire.

Barford had a unit of the East Surrey Yeomanry from early March 1915 for a couple of weeks. One of the troops billeted here was Robert Cook. He served with C Squadron, Surrey Yeomanry at Gallipoli and on the Western Front. In an interview with the Imperial War Museum, in 1984, he stated that he was posted to C Squadron in Stratford upon Avon and Barford from January to March 1915. He learned to ride during his time here. He remembered that the people with whom the soldiers were billeted in Barford were only paid 10d per day but they nevertheless were provided with wonderful food.

He and his unit grew very fond of Barford and to avoid upsetting their new friends they arranged to leave in the middle of the night when the order came for them to move on. However the word had gone around the village and despite it being a cold and wet night nearly the whole village turned out with lanterns and shouted, "God speed, come home safe to Barford." The soldiers were so moved by this that these words became their war cry whenever they went over the top. No doubt that, for some of these brave men, these were the last words they heard.

Robert Cook was sent from Barford to Alexandria, Egypt in 1915.

During the soldiers' time here Mrs Smith-Ryland made the Ryland Hall available for evening recreation.

## Belgian refugees

Commencing in September 1914, over three hundred thousand Belgian refugees began arriving in Britain. In November 1914 a small number of these refugees arrived in Barford. Mr Dennis Smith-Ryland provided a house for them, in Church Street.

A committee was formed to look after the new arrivals. The members of this committee were: E Hemmings, Ernest Chadwick, William Bacon, Mrs E Hemmings, Mrs H Reading, Mrs John Archer and Mrs Andrews. Mr John Archer was the secretary. Many villagers loaned furniture and food was supplied as well. There is no record of any refugees attending the school, but a concert was given by one of the Belgians in the Church. It is likely that the refugees remained in the village for some time. The last of them did not depart from the area until the end of the War in 1918.

## Red Cross Hospital at Barford Hill

As early as May 1912 practices were held by the Barford and Wellesbourne detachments of the British Red Cross Society (No 9 and No 14 of the Voluntary Aid Detachment) in preparation for the war. The Red Cross Hospital at Longbridge Manor, home of Major Airth-Richardson, opened on 1st December 1914. By the end of March 1915 it was full of patients. Dennis Smith-Ryland offered Barford Hill House as a VAD Red Cross Hospital and the medical facility at Longbridge was transferred there on 31st March 1915. The new hospital was under the control of the First Southern General Hospital.

The commandant in charge was Mrs Smith-Ryland. The hospital stores were at Watchbury House, managed by Mrs Kenward Barker. Nurses came to work at the hospital from all over the country, including Daphne Trevor from Lathbury in Buckinghamshire, who earned respect for her kindness and devotion.

Sadly some of the patients did not survive. Among these was William Lodwick from Carmarthen, Wales. He had been wounded in France. William was the son of Timothy Lodwick, Llanelly, Carmarthen. He was aged 28 when he died in Barford, on 31st December 1916. He was a driver. Perhaps Richard Jones, the head gardener at Barford Hill, who came from North Wales, visited him.

The local 'ladies' generally staffed the Red Cross Hospitals as it was not considered suitable work for the working class.

Donations of vegetables, pheasants, cakes and rabbits were acknowledged in the local newspapers.

During the war up to thirty-two patients were treated at any one time. The Royal Automobile Club organised the transport of the injured troops from Warwick train station to Barford, using privately owned cars. In April 1917 the patients were taken to the Jephson Gardens in Leamington, to join over a thousand troops at a garden party and fete held in their honour. A vaudeville entertainment was provided and the Band of the Royal Warwickshire Regiment played a selection of popular music.

Mrs Airth-Richardson and Miss E Anderson were honoured by the Joint War Committee of the British Red Cross and the Order of St John of Jerusalem at the end of the War. Mrs Smith-Ryland was honoured with an OBE.

Group of patients and nurses at Barford Red Cross Hospital.

Mrs Edith Smith-Ryland

## Military Service Tribunals

The Military Service Act, passed by the Government in 1916, specified that all single men between the ages of 16 and 40 were liable to be called up for military service. The law was soon changed to include married men and the age limit was raised to 51.

Military Service Tribunals were formed by borough, urban district and rural district councils to hear applications for exemption from conscription into the British Army during WWI. Men could apply for exemption on the grounds of doing work of national importance, business or domestic hardship, medical unfitness, and conscientious objection. Local Tribunals were set up in Warwick and Stratford upon Avon.

At the Warwick Rural District Tribunal in July 1916, Alfred William Ireland, aged 33, was granted an exemption until January 1917, as he was the only baker in Barford. Also in July 1916, Barford Electrical Company applied for an exemption for its fitter, Walter Brindley. Lieutenant Hamilton pointed out that the electrical works had only recently started and was for the benefit of very few people. Barford Electrical Company Manager stated that Brindley was "an invalid, more or less". Lieutenant Hamilton replied that all mechanics were wanted for the army. An exemption was granted only until 1st August 1916.

William Inson also applied for an exemption at this time for his son, aged 23. Mr Inson stated that his son helped him in hay carting and in scavenging work. His son had been medically passed for garrison duty, at home. An exemption was granted to him until 1st October 1916. In May 1916 an application was submitted on behalf of Ernest Worrall, who was the only one left of the four men working as smiths in Barford before the War. Ernest Worrall was working for twenty farmers in the neighbourhood. A conditional exemption was agreed to. The 'conditional exemption' is very likely to have been that Ernest remained in his present occupation.

Those with a conditional exemption, as this was, had a better chance of remaining at home but there was no guarantee of not being called-up.

At a meeting of a Tribunal, on 14th June 1918, at which Mr J W Ryland presided, the Clerk, Mr C J Passman, announced that by proclamation that day the exemptions of all men employed in agricultural work were cancelled and applications for exemption on that ground could not be considered by that Tribunal.

The National Service Representative, Mr S Douglas, opposed the renewal of exemption certificates in the following cases:

Thomas Moore, aged 43, employed on the Barford Hill Estate in tree felling and preparing material for farm work. Mr R Jones, the estate agent, said Moore felled trees for pit propping and was adapted for the work he was now doing. The Chairman responded, "That's no good". with the Clerk adding "There are any number of men in the county could do this work. We have no power to grant exemption." On Moore stating his domestic difficulties, the Chairman said, "That does not count, we have come to the extremes now."

John Hadley

John Hadley, a butcher in Barford aged 43, was granted one month's temporary exemption in 1916. However, in August 1918 the case of two master butchers at Barford, John Hadley and F D Lees were considered together. Lees was putting in four days a week at munitions work and it was suggested that Hadley should look after Lees business. The Tribunal decided to send Lees into the army and ordered Hadley to carry on Lees business for the benefit of the latter's mother.

William A Bacon, aged 46, plumber and decorator, who had lost all his nine employees since the War started, said that he did work for the VAD Hospital at Barford. He was refused exemption, but twenty-eight days were allowed before he was called up.

## Barford Electrical Light Supply Company

Barford Electrical Light Supply Company was founded in 1914 to use the ancient corn mill to produce hydro-electricity. The Leamington Courier reported on this in February 1915:

***Barford now has a system of light supply. All the cables have been laid underground. Eleven cast iron standards with ornamental tops and concave reflectors have been fixed in suitable places. These lamps give one hundred candle power and the effect is to give Barford a brilliant appearance which London would no doubt much like to possess. Some of the larger houses in the village also enjoy electricity at this time.***

James Hemmings owned the Barford Water Mill. His son Richard William Hemmings (1898-1971) served with the Royal Navy. He enlisted in 1917 and served on HMS President and also on the Withnoe, an aircraft storage unit and training ship.

## Women and their role during the Great War

Victorian values were still very much adhered to at the start of the War. Women of all classes were expected to take care of household duties, either through service or supervising the servants. This was as true in Barford as anywhere else in the country.

Daisy, Countess of Warwick, writing in the Stratford Herald in July 1915, was concerned that the new dress lengths were showing too much ankle and that some ankles were not designed to be seen, ever! She also cautioned ladies to choose carefully the dress that 'one would wear when one was having one's portrait painted' to make sure it was a full-length gown.

Miss Eleanor Archer was unusual in having the position of 'Overseer of the Poor and Census Collector' in Barford. She also wrote social articles, describing weddings, balls and parties, for the local newspapers. In addition she was involved in improving the health education of women, particularly their reproductive health, and in training them for employment, such as working in a dairy. She even opened an employment exchange for women in Warwick.

So women did what they were allowed to do to help the war effort. They set up sewing circles. Mrs Pepys, at Plestowes, was in charge of the Barford circle. By the end of November 1914, the ladies had sent twenty pairs of socks, nine belts, six mufflers, six helmets and twelve pairs of mittens to the Warwickshire Yeomanry. An acknowledgement was received from Lady French, lady-in-waiting to the Queen.

A committee was set up and concerts were held at the Ryland Hall to provide funds for the Barford War Comforts Supply Room.

A 'Tipperary Room' was opened at the Working Men's Club to provide a space for the wives and girlfriends of serving soldiers to socialise. They could not, at this time, appear unescorted in public.

In early 1915 the District Council organised the training of ladies in the art of milking and other 'easy' farm work. At this time also women started to be employed as railway clerks.

By June 1915 it was reported that some of the village girls had migrated to Coventry to assist in the making of munitions. Some of the men had joined them.

It was not until the end of March 1917 that the Women's Land Army was set up. Girls and women in every class of society responded. The land girls were paid 18s. per week. An outfit of high boots, breeches, two overalls and hat was supplied free. Volunteers had to work where the Board of Agriculture sent them. During the first few months the women met with discouragement through the prejudice of farmers and the uncertain demand for their labour. At first they undertook light farm work but as time went on they undertook the heaviest labour. The winter of 1918 was very severe and food rationing was introduced. The items rationed were sugar, meat, jam, bread, butter, margarine and lard. By August 1918 farmers appeared to be more accepting of women's help on their farms. Rationing of meat continued until December 1919. The Women's Land Army was disbanded on 30th November 1919.

## Entertainment in Barford during the War

APC Concert February 1917 as reported in the Leamington Spa Courier:

***A very successful concert was given on Thursday last week at the Ryland Hall, when owing to the initiative of Mrs Hewitt, the Army Pay Corps Male Choir kindly came from Warwick to supply the entire programme. There was a good attendance, though, owing to the inclement weather, several ticket holders were unable to be present. The Male Choir, living up to their reputation of excellence, gave a delightful concert. The part songs, under the able conductorship of Sergeant Pickering, were perfection of correct and well trained singing, particularly "The Pilgrim's Progress" chorus from "Tannhauser" and the "Christian Martyrs". "Annie Laurie" seemed to be the general favourite, for the admirable blending of the voices made the old Scotch air something new and fascinating. Pte F S Dunn charmed his hearers with "Macushla" and "Sincerity" for which he was deservedly encored. Pte G Neale Peck, who, by the way, is a new addition to the choir, delighted the audience with his singing. His rendering of "There's Only One England" with the choir taking up the chorus, was something to be remembered. Sergeants J B Page and F S Pickering contributed a vocal duet, entitled "Anchored" which was a distinct success. Pte W Saxon, as violinist, and Corporals F H Brooks and K Williams as pianists, were all excellent, their contribution being much enjoyed. Last but not least was Sergeant Glaysher, the humorist, whose funny selections caused uproars of laughter, needless to add he was encored vociferously for each song. At the conclusion the Rector, the Rev Ingham Brooke, in thanking the visitors for their kindness in coming to Barford, spoke of the pleasant evening he had spent making special mention of the part songs, and then called for three cheers for the performers, which were heartily given. Sergeant Cogswell, the choir's popular secretary, suitably responded. The balance sheet proves very satisfactory, quite a substantial sum being handed over to the Barford War Comforts Supply Room.***

**Party for families of men in active service, December 1918**

The Leamington Spa Courier reported on this event:

***Through the kindness of a few friends a delightful tea was spread on Wednesday evening in the Rifle Range and the guests included the fathers, mothers, and children of the brave Barford men who are now in active service. A concert was also thoroughly enjoyed. Master B and Miss N Hammond with piano and violin rendered excellent service, their efforts being much appreciated. Mrs Tomlinson, Mr Bacon and Miss Edna Hewitt also did well. Mr Whetters (from Grove Fields) and Mr Bradshaw (from Warwick) most readily came and gave much pleasure to the company with songs and other amusing contributions. At the close of the entertainment Mr J Hemmings proposed a hearty vote of thanks to those that had contributed to the success of the evening.***

**Coursing**

Coursing meetings were held regularly during the years of the First World War at Debden in Barford. Most of the participating owners were not from the village.

The meetings were reported in the Coventry Evening Telegraph, such as this report in November 1915:

***A boisterous wind, accompanied by continuous showers, made matters none too pleasant for visitors to the Barford coursing fixture. Sport, however, was excellent, for though hares naturally run wild, they were so plentiful that they were brought forward in nice sequence and a series of interesting courses were covered. Three of the stakes were divided by Kinver Kennel and a very enthusiastic Birmingham courser in Mr A C Frost took a share in two. The dog James Stapleton, after running his first course, was purchased by Mr H C Pulwell of Wappenbury, the subsequent division making him quite a cheap purchase. The winning prize was £8 and second prize £4.***

Warwickshire Yeomanry Comforts Fund benefited by over £25 from this particular meeting.

**Hunting** was popular before most of the horses were requisitioned for war use.

Yeomanry sports in Warwickshire

The King commands me to assure you of the true sympathy of His Majesty and The Queen in your sorrow.

He whose loss you mourn died in the noblest of causes. His Country will be ever grateful to him for the sacrifice he has made for Freedom and Justice.

Milner

*Secretary of State for War.*

# THE FALLEN

## 242326 Private Francis Hubert Freeman

## C Company, 2nd/6th Battalion, Royal Warwickshire Regiment

Francis was born in 1889 in Warwick, the son of Joseph, a groom, and Frances Freeman, of Watchbury Cottage, 6 High Street Barford. He had a sister, Rose, and worked as a gardener. He also had a brother, Herbert Arthur, who survived the War. Herbert lived with his family in Keytes Lane.

Francis married Sarah Louise Rudman of Alderham Cottages, Barford before enlisting in Warwick.

He served overseas at some time after 1st January 1916.

He was killed in action during the attack on the Schuler Galleries on Sunday 26th August 1917, aged 28.

He was awarded the British War Medal and the Victory Medal.

## 10607 Private George Hiorns

## South Staffordshire Regiment

George Hiorns was born in March 1876 in Barford to William and Mary Hiorns. He had an older brother, William, and three sisters, Louisa, Ada and Lucy. They lived at Longbridge Cottage, Sherbourne.

After leaving school he became a paper carrier but, wanting to improve his lot, he enlisted in December 1894 at Warwick with the South Staffordshire Regiment, as 4419 Private, aged 18, and was sent to Lichfield for training.

In January 1897 he was posted to India for five years and then to the Boer War in South Africa. He completed his period of engagement in January 1903 and was discharged on to the Army Reserve. His first discharge came in December 1906.

George married Annie Matilda Chambers and they lived at 88 Cliffe Hill, Warwick and had two sons, Cecil and Walter.
In 1911 he worked as an estate labourer at Wasperton.

In October 1914 George re-enlisted at Warwick with the South Staffordshire Regiment and he was sent to France in 1915.

On January 30th 1916 his battalion moved into the Bray-sur-Somme area and were under shellfire for several days. George sustained injuries and died of his wounds on February 4th 1916, aged, 39.

He is buried at Chipilly Communal Cemetery, Somme.
He was awarded the British War Medal and the Victory Medal and Star.

# 103244 Private Harry William Reeve

# Machine Gun Corps (Infantry)

Harry was born in 1886 in Lighthorne to Willam and Jane Reeve. He had five sisters, Elizabeth, Elda, Winifred, Mary and Jane, and the family lived at Fir Tree Hill, Charlecote where Harry and William worked as waggoners on a local farm.

Harry married Rebecca Jane and had a son in 1905 and they lived in High Street, Barford.

He enlisted as 24176 in the Royal Wales Regiment later transferring to the Machine Gun Corps.

He was killed in action during the Flanders Offensive at Ypres on 25th October 1917, aged 31.

He is commemorated on the Tyne Cot Memorial, Belgium.

He was awarded the British War Medal and the Victory Medal.

## 202684 Private Harry Woodward

## Princess Charlotte of Wales's Royal Berkshire Regiment

Harry was born in 1886 in Dorsington to John Woodward, an agricultural labourer, and his wife Agnes. He had two brothers, Nellesford and Frank, and three sisters, Maisie, Eva and Blanche.

In 1901 he worked as a farm boy at Lodge Farm, Snitterfield and later as a gardener at Barford Hill House.

When he enlisted he lived with his wife Ellen in Bridge Street, Barford.

He was killed in action on 4th June 1917, aged 31.

He is buried in the Hermies Hill British Cemetery, Pas de Calais, France.

He was awarded the British War Medal and the Victory Medal.

# 13940 Private John Smith MM

## Prince Albert's Somerset Light Infantry

John Smith was born in 1892 in Kineton to Alfred Smith, a farm labourer, and Amy, neé Reason. He had five brothers, Ernest, Wilfred, Thomas, Alfred and William, and three sisters, Amy, Lily and Kate. The family lived in Church Street, Barford, although they had lived in several local villages where some of the children were born.

John enlisted to the 7th Battalion at Leamington and served in France. He was awarded the Military Medal for bravery in the field but was killed in action during the Battle of Transloy on 1st October 1916, aged 24.

He is commemorated on the Thiepval Memorial, Somme, France.

Other medals he received were the Star, the British War Medal and the Victory Medal.

# Nurse Muriel Mary Graham

## Voluntary Aid Detachment, British Red Cross

Muriel was born in Oxfordshire in 1895, the daughter of Hugh Graham and Jessie Graham, who was a wealthy American. She had two brothers, Alastair and Hugh, and an older sister Sybil.

Muriel's father, Hugh Graham (1860 – 1921), was the son of Sir Richard Graham of Scotland. The Graham family came to live in Barford House in 1911. Alastair, Muriel's brother, became a friend of the novelist Evelyn Waugh at Oxford University.

Muriel was educated at home in Barford by a governess. Like all the Graham family she enjoyed her time in the village, hunting and attending the Warwick Hunt Ball.

In 1914 it is likely that she helped her father organise a lavish ball for three hundred and fifty-one guests in Warwick Town Hall in aid of Warneford Hospital.

She enrolled in the Warwick 144 Red Cross Detachment in February 1913. From January 1915 she was a nurse at the Warren VAD Hospital in Leamington.

She died of acute meningitis on 7th December 1918, aged 23, in London.

She was awarded the Royal Red Cross 2nd Division.

## 15976 Reuben Barnbrook

## Royal Warwickshire Regiment

Reuben was born in November 1895 to Charles Barnbrook, a bricklayer, and his wife Elizabeth (Bessie), a laundress, who lived on Wellesbourne Road., Barford. He had six brothers and sisters, Ernest, Harry, Thomas, Sarah, Lucy and Sidney.

Reuben worked as a ploughboy on a local farm.

On 16th January 1915, aged 19, he enlisted as a driver with the Royal Regiment of Artillery.

He served for twenty-three weeks but spent twenty weeks in hospital with bronchitis, with which he had suffered before he enlisted. The medical officer declared that he had evidence of destructive tubercular disease of the right lung and that he would never make an efficient soldier, so recommended discharge on health grounds. He was discharged on 6th June 1915.

Subsequently he re-enlisted with the 1st Battalion Royal Warwickshire Regiment and was sent to France where he was killed in action, aged 21, on 12th October 1916 at the Battle of Le Transloy.

Reuben Barnbrook was awarded the Victory Medal and the British War Medal.

He is commemorated at the Thiepval Memorial, Somme, France.

## 104796 Private Francis Henry Talbot

## Royal Warwickshire Regiment/Devon Regiment

Francis was born in Barford in 1897 to Henry and Elizabeth Talbot who lived at 2 Bridge Street. Henry was a coachman at Barford House.

After Francis left school he became a market gardener.

He enlisted in the Royal Warwickshire Regiment as a reservist on 7th December 1915 and was mobilised on 12th May 1916.
He transferred to the Devon Regiment in the Labour Battalion as 58299 Private on 8th March 1917 and was posted to France on 22nd March 1917 as part of the British Expeditionary Force.

On 26th January 1918 he was discharged to a base hospital after being injured two days earlier, but rejoined his unit on 29th January and was back in the field on 1st February.

Francis Henry Talbot was killed in action 21st March 1918, aged 21.
He is commemorated on the Pozieres Memorial, Somme, France and also on the Memorial Screen in Barford Church.

He was awarded the Victory Medal and the British War Medal.

## DM2/154392 Lance Corporal William Carter

## Royal Army Service Corps

William was born in Derby in 1896 to William Carter junior, a miller, and his wife Hannah.

He had an older sister, Mabel, and two brothers, Leslie and Ernest. William worked as a journeyman baker. The family lived in Church Street, Barford.

William enlisted with the Royal Army Service Corps and was sent to Belgium where he was killed in action at Lijssenthoek on 25th April 1918, aged 22.

He is buried at Lijssenthoek Military Cemetery.

He was awarded the British War Medal and the Victory Medal.

## 35667 Albert Edward Winston

## Worcestershire Regiment

Albert Winston was born in Barford in 1892, the son of Alfred Winston, a butcher, and Sarah Winston.

After he left school he became a house decorator. On 16th November 1914 he married Florence Helena Robinson from Llanelly. They lived in Yew Tree Cottage on Wellesbourne Road, Barford. In December 1915 they had a daughter, Dora Agnes.

Albert enlisted on 28th August 1916 as a machine gunner in the Worcestershire Regiment and later the Machine Gun corps where his service number was 84886.

He served in France and Flanders and was killed in action on 21st March 1918, aged 26.

Albert was awarded the Victory Medal and the War Medal in 1922.

His wife was awarded a pension of 20s. 5d. a week. She later remarried a Mr Gardiner.

## 20152 Private Arthur Hopkins

## 11th Battalion, Royal Warwickshire Regiment

Arthur was born in Willersley, Herefordshire, the son of Henry, an agricultural labourer, and Mary, née Hopkins. He had four brothers, James, Henry, Caleb and Ralph, and a sister, Alice. The family later lived at Mickleton.

Arthur married Lizzie Reeves, aged 36, from Keytes Lane, Barford, on June 2nd 1909. Sadly she died on 17th March 1910 and is buried in Barford churchyard. After her death he lived with a friend and worked as a building labourer.

Arthur joined the Royal Warwickshire Regiment and was sent to France where he was killed in action on 20th January 1917, aged 33.

He is buried in the Longuenesse Souvenir Cemetery, Pas de Calais, St Omer, France.

He was awarded the British War Medal and the Victory Medal.

## 322064 Private Charles Wesley Hunt, Pioneer
## 19th Division Signal Company, Royal Engineers

Charles Hunt was born in Barford in 1894 to Charles William Hunt, who was a market gardener, and his wife Esther Ann Hunt. He had two younger brothers Albert and Ernest. They lived on the Wellesbourne Road. Charles Wesley Hunt was a member of the Barford Fife and Drum Band.

Charles became a gardener and moved to Fairford, Gloucestershire. He married Lizzie Law on 26th December 1917 at the Baptist Church, Fairford.

They moved to Barford where his wife ran the Post Office and he became a GPO engineer. They had a daughter, Edna May, on 10th November 1918, three months after he was killed.

He enlisted in Coventry in 1915, at the age of 22, into No 4 Signal Section, 19th Division Signal Company, Royal Engineers. He served overseas some time after January 1st 1916.

Charles was killed in action on Sunday 25th August 1918, aged 25.

He is buried in Le Vertannoy British Cemetery, Hinges, Pas de Calais, France.

He was awarded the British War Medal and the Victory Medal on 20th March 1922.

He is commemorated on the Memorial Screen in Barford Church.

Lizzie, his wife, was awarded a pension of thirteen shillings and nine pence a week.

## Captain Henry Dennis Smith-Ryland
## 1st Warwickshire Yeomanry, Household Cavalry,
## Imperial Camel Corps

Henry Dennis Smith-Ryland (commonly known as Dennis) was born in 1891 to Charles Alston and Edith Smith-Ryland who lived at Barford Hill House. He had a younger brother, Charles Ivor, and three sisters, Evelyn, Adria Noel and Kitty.

On the death of his father in 1914 Dennis took over his duties managing the estate and taking part in village life. He organised a house for Belgian refugees in the village and allowed Barford Hill House to be used as a Red Cross Hospital. He was engaged to Enid Petrie who lived in London.

Dennis enlisted and served in Egypt with the Imperial Camel Corps. He died of his wounds on 7th April 1917, aged 26.

He is buried in the Kantara Memorial Cemetery, Egypt.

His Memorial Service at Sherbourne Church was attended by a large number of people from Barford and Sherbourne.

He was awarded the Star, the British War Medal and the Victory Medal.

## 45504 Lance Corporal Frank Albert Baker
## Princess Charlotte of Wales's Royal Berkshire Regiment

Frank was born in Barford in 1900, the only son of Edward Baker, a gardener, who lived on High Street with his wife Agnes and three daughters, Kate, Iris and Margaret.

He enlisted in Leamington Spa and initially served as 11932, Devonshire Regiment.

Frank served overseas from 1st January 1916 but was killed in action at the Battle of the Hindenburg Line on Tuesday 17th September 1918, aged 18.

He is buried at St Emilie Valley Cemetery, Villers-Faucon, Somme, France.

He was awarded the British War Medal and the Victory Medal.

## 10918 Private Frederick Bartlett

## Machine Gun Corps (Infantry)

Frederick was born in 1893 in Barford, the son of James Bartlett, a gardener, who lived in Keytes Lane with his wife Elizabeth and five other children, Arthur, Ephraim, Charlie, Annie and Florence. When Frederick was very young his mother died. James remarried another Elizabeth and had three more daughters, Ethel, Ellen and Edith.

He enlisted in Coventry and served overseas after 1st January 1916. He formerly served as R/16742, Kings Royal Rifle Corps.

Frederick Bartlett was killed in action on Saturday 31st May 1918, aged 26.

He is commemorated on the Soissons Memorial, Aisne, France.

He was awarded the British War Medal and the Victory Medal.

## 14800 Private Frederick J Pilkington

## Kings (Liverpool) Regiment

Frederick Pilkington was born in 1892, the son of Ada Pilkington, née Farmer, in Surrey. He was probably named after his grandfather Frederick Gardener. His mother was from Latham Gardens, Ormskirk in Lancashire. In 1901 he was staying with his grandmother Deborah Farmer at 4 High Street, Barford, He worked as a gardener in Warwick after he left school.

Frederick enlisted to the 4th (Extra Reserve) Battalion, King's (Liverpool) Regiment, 98th Brigade, 33rd Division at Southport.

He arrived in France on Saturday 24th July 1915, as part of the British Expeditionary Force.

He was wounded on 3rd September 1916. Four days later he was sent home to England to recover. He returned to France on 28th February 1917.

Frederick Pilkington was killed in action during the Flanders Offensive on Tuesday 16th April 1918, aged 26.

He is commemorated on the Ploegsteert Memorial, Comines-Warneton, Hainaut, Belgium, for soldiers with no known grave.

He is also commemorated on the Memorial Screen in Barford Church.

He was awarded the Star, the British War Medal and the Victory Medal.

## 52211 William Powers

## 15th Battalion, Royal Irish Rifles

William Powers was born in Wasperton in 1894, the son of George Powers, a herdsman, and Sophia. His brother John also enlisted but survived.

At the time of enlisting William was working in Barford, for William Canning at Debden Farm.

He was a rifleman with the 15th Battalion, Royal Irish Rifles.

He died on the 31st May 1918, aged 24, from wounds sustained near Calais, France.

William Powers is commemorated at the Esquelbecq Military Cemetery, Calais, France.

He is also commemorated on the Memorial Screen in Wasperton Church.

William was awarded the British War Medal and the Victory Medal.

# THE MEN WHO RETURNED TO BARFORD

**Some of the men who returned home safely had amazing stories to tell and had to live with awful memories. Many found it too painful to speak of their wartime experiences, even to their families.**

When the men retuned home on leave they often had to be subjected to very strong disinfectant and insect killer before they were allowed to enter their homes.

## Lieutenant Charles Ivor Phipson Smith-Ryland

## Coldstream Guards/Warwickshire Yeomanry

Charles Ivor Phipson Smith-Ryland was born in 1898 to Charles Alston and Edith Smith Ryland. He enlisted in the Coldstream Guards and was wounded in France in 1916. He was admitted to the hospital at Eton House, but was later discharged. In 1918 he was a lieutenant, Reserve of Officers in the Warwickshire Hussars, Territorial Army. This battalion was part of the Warwickshire Yeomanry. Charles left active service in 1920.

He married Leila Tollemache at the Coldstream Guards Chapel, Wellington Barracks, London, in 1919. His brother-in-law, Rev H Gibb, who had lost his sight in active service, gave the address at his wedding. Five bridesmaids dressed in 'love in a mist' blue chiffon with silver waistbelts and blue veils trimmed with silver attended the bride. Charles and Leila had two children, June, in 1924 and Charles Mortimer, in 1927. Charles was appointed a magistrate for Warwickshire in 1923 and nominated as Sheriff of Warwickshire in 1925.

Captain Charles Ivor Phipson Smith-Ryland was found shot in the grounds of Barford Hill House on the 27th of December 1929 by Arthur Workman, a labourer, aged 17. He died later that day. The coroner recorded a verdict of accidental death.

He was awarded the British War Medal and the Victory Medal.

## Private Harry Vincent Penn

## Grenadier Guards

Harry Vincent Penn was born in Baxterley, Warwickshire, on 7th October 1896 to Charlotte Ann Penn. He was one of those who enlisted as soon as he could. When they moved to Barford, Vincent lived with his uncle and aunt, Edmund and Mary Keyte of Wellesbourne Road. The Keyte family were carpenters, market gardeners and shopkeepers. He attended Barford School. By 1911 Vincent had left school and was working as a commercial gardener and still living with the Keyte family.

Aged 18, he enlisted with the Grenadier Guards as a drummer boy and was sent to France where on 30th October 1914, at the first Battle of Ypres, he was with the Guards. They had been sent along with the Scots Guards and Hussars to reinforce the 3rd Cavalry Division on the ridge of Zandvoorde under the command of General Byng.

The Germans were bombarding the British with heavy guns whilst the British had only light field guns. The telephone wires were cut between the firing line and Brigade HQ again and again, necessitating messages to be sent by runners. Harry Vincent Penn undertook this most dangerous duty, traversing an open field pitted with craters, passing through crumbling farm buildings, crossing the road to Zillebeke, and making his way along fifty yards of ditch and across an open ploughed field to Zillebeke Wood, which was being raked by German artillery searching for British field guns.

After leaving the wood, Penn had to cross an open field to HQ. The brave lad made this journey several times that day, crawling or running where ground afforded little cover and though shells were bursting all around him, on each occasion coming through unscathed. The attack continued until dusk and then the German infantry advanced on foot but were met by fierce fire from the British infantry and field guns. Just as the situation looked most dangerous the Germans melted away.

Drummer Vincent Penn was awarded the Distinguished Conduct Medal ***'For conspicuous gallantry in carrying messages all day under very heavy shell fire from the firing line to HQ and doing admirable work on many occasions.'***

King George V, at Hazebrouk Railway Station, North France, presented him with his medal on 3rd December 1914.

After the war he married Ethel Needle in Warwick and later lived at the Fire Station in Moseley, Birmingham, and then at 17 Culham Road. He died, aged 86 in December 1982.

His mother married Gilbert Higgett, a saddler and harness maker. They had two sons, Edmund Gilbert born in 1909, and Walter Charles born in 1912, who lived in Barford all their lives. Edmund later went on to serve in WWII.

## John Powers

## Gloucestershire Regiment

John Powers was the younger son of George, a herdsman, and Sophie Powers of Wasperton. He had two sisters, Rose and Emily, and an older brother William. At the time of enlisting, John worked as a stable lad at Charlecote Park. He hoped to join the Horse Guard Regiment but he was put into the Gloucester Regiment.

John was posted to France in August 1917. He started his journey to France at Harwich and landed at the Hook of Holland. Soon after arriving he was captured at Arleux. He was declared missing in April 1918. John had been taken as a prisoner of war. He escaped from the camp four times but was recaptured each time. After this he was sent to Germany and put to work on building the railway into the Krupp Iron and Steel works. Often while laying the tracks the prisoners were bombed and strafed by the British Air Force. Some of the German guards had compassion for the prisoners and would 'accidentally' drop a loaf of bread when loading the supply trains, put their foot on it and break it so it was not fit for the German soldiers to eat. The prisoners were glad of any food. At the end of the war John and the other prisoners were released and returned to England. The first thing he saw on arrival at Warwick was the advertisement for Bisto gravy. He returned home to Wasperton in early 1919 wearing his prisoner of war cap with a small piece of bread tucked inside it. When he arrived in Wasperton his parents were in bed but on hearing the latch of the gate and the familiar footsteps his mother exclaimed, "That's our Jack!" John married Constance Bradbrook in 1928.

John always insisted he was not a hero, just an ordinary person doing his bit for his country.

He was awarded the British War Medal, the Victory Medal and the King's Medal.

John Powers died in 1972 and is buried in Barford.

## Ernest Byerley

## Horse Guards Regiment

Ernest was a gardener like his father Joseph, who was head gardener at Barford House. His mother Annie née Ward was a member of an old Wasperton family.

He was born at Wasperton. The Byerley family were among the best gardeners in the area, frequently wining prizes for their produce at local shows.
Ernest had a brother, Frederick, and a sister, Elsie Annie, who died as a baby.

Ernest was eighteen when he enlisted in the army in Warwick in December 1915. He went to enlist with his good friend John Powers. While in the army Ernest collected cigarette silks and his mother made a beautiful picture by sewing a large number of these rare silks around a photograph of Ernest in uniform.

Ernest returned from the War to live in Wasperton. He died in Warwick in 1970.

## Wenman 'Kit' Wykeham-Musgrave

Wenman 'Kit' Wykeham-Musgrave was born in Barford, the son of Wenman and Gertrude Wykeham-Musgrave. He had three sisters, Lettice, Monica and Janice, who were educated at home by Lilian Hunter, a governess. Kit was educated at the Royal Naval College, Isle of Wight, and at Britannia Naval College in Devon. Subsequently he became a commander in the Royal Navy.

Kit Wykeham-Musgrave has the distinction of having survived being torpedoed on three different ships on the same day, 22nd September 1914. While he was a midshipman aboard the HMS Aboukir a German U-boat attacked them. He went overboard when this ship was going down and swam to HMS Hogue. This ship was then torpedoed. He swam to HMS Cressey as it was torpedoed. He managed to cling on to a piece of driftwood until a Dutch trawler rescued him. This all happened in the space of one hour.

Wenman Wykeham-Musgrave re-joined the navy in 1939 and reached the rank of commander. He died in 1989.

# Major Robert Airth Richardson

## 1st Warwickshire Yeomanry

Robert Airth Richardson was an engineer. He lived at Longbridge Manor with his wife Elizabeth and daughters, Daphne, Phyllis, Marjorie, Patricia and Yvonne. He had an engineering business in Warwick. Robert and his wife were born in Northern Ireland. He was aged 49 when he joined the army.

In May 1915, he was promoted from major to brevet lieutenant colonel in recognition of his distinguished service and gallant conduct on the occasion of a serious explosion on the transport ship Wayfarer. Two men and five horses were killed but the rest of the two hundred crew, all Warwickshire Yeomanry, and seven hundred and sixty-nine horses were brought to safely at Cobh in Ireland.

Major Airth Richardson was heavily involved in village affairs in Barford, attending parish meetings. His wife Elizabeth was one of the nurses in charge of Barford Hill Red Cross Hospital for the duration of the War.

Robert Airth Richardson died in 1936.

## Captain Joshua Rupert Ingham Brooke

## Royal Garrison Artillery

Joshua Rupert Ingham Brooke, son of Rev William Ingham Brooke, became an agriculturalist after attending Balliol College, Oxford. He was a captain in the Royal Garrison Artillery and was awarded the MBE in June 1919. Joshua was also awarded a Medal for Military Merit, 4th Class, from Greece, for distinguished services rendered during the course of the campaign. He married Margaret Hewett in 1923. Captain Ingham Brooke died in a nursing home in Ipswich, Suffolk, in 1934, aged 41.

## Corporal Bernard Rice

Bernard Rice was a member of Barford Rifle Club. He was the son of Edward Rice, a physician, of Stratford upon Avon and he was born in Oxford in 1891. Bernard wrote many letters from the trenches in France to his aunt Emily, who lived in Stratford upon Avon. He writes of his diet of bully beef, biscuits, jam and tea. Water was often in scarce supply. He requested a supply of knitted socks ***'as socks are rotting after three days in the cold, muddy water of the trenches'.***

In June 1915 he writes:

***By this time it was just dusk, and the firework effect of the battle now raging at its height was really very fine. The actual trench lines were hidden from our view by intervening hills and woods, but the heavy shells of the enemy could be seen distinctly bursting at various points as they searched the most likely place to find our heavy artillery. The whole scene was lighted by this weird bluish glare of their star shells, which kept rising above the line of hills and woods and hanging for a moment only to plunge downwards once more, describing the most elegant curves of fire. At various points great vivid streaks would shoot upwards, ever broadening until lost in the general reflection in the sky above,***

*denoting the burst of some enemy shell of heavy weight and at frequent intervals one would see a lightening flash dart downwards amongst the trees, showing the burst of shrapnel. It was a queer sensation wondering how it was faring over there, and how big the casualty list would be in the papers that week.*

*I was beginning to wonder where our good commander in chief would be and what he would be doing. It was nearly four hours since the show started and it had quietened down considerably.*

*Suddenly in our rear, far away in the distance, a bright light twinkled, disappeared, and reappeared again, a little closer. I remember drowsily thinking it might be the general's car approaching when another came into view and another, until there must have been a hundred little twinkling lights all bobbing and twisting about in a long snaky line one behind the other. Very soon a huge Daimler bus charged through the now deserted street, quickly followed by others looking very huge and ominous in the darkness.*

*"Reinforcements." said someone. I happened to be with our 'heavies' when the show started and it looked pretty exciting, I can tell you. The ground fairly shook and the reports of bursting shells merged into one continuous crash, which was simply deafening. It startled us all a bit, for I, for one, had never heard such a savage outburst of firing before, not even on the Aisne.*

*We could see the ridge along which some of the shells were bursting and it was just one sheet of vivid flame.*

*However anyone could have the nerve to stick there, even in a trench, I don't know. Soon the fire shifted further upon the line to the real point of the intended attack and they tossed over half a dozen big shells to put wind up our heavy gunners, who had become rather active and I cleared out with my despatches for the column! It was getting late and the light was failing, so the old girl and I pushed along. On arriving at the village I was surprised to see a crowd of villagers standing on the road just clear of the houses and on the neighbouring banks. Everyone it seemed had 'properly got the wind up'; old women were crying; the younger ones looking anxious and wan; and all seized on me for news.*

Friends from Barford who all fought together

Vinn Penn

Dear Lucy we are safe & sound once more thank the Lord but a lot of poor souls have gone under. We could hear them in the distance but they did not reach us. We have not heard from Vin since 11th of this month but trust he is safe. Hoping you are all quite well. With much love from loving sister Emma.

Cigarette silks Ernest Byerley sent to his mother which she mounted around his photograph

Star, British War Medal, Victory Medal

Charles Wesley Hunt's WWI drum used in the Barford Drum & Fife Band.

# WORLD WAR II

# World War II

Desperation, anxiety, sadness – words used to describe Barford during the years of WWII but there was also fun and action for children. This was a lively village at that time with shops, a busy school, large houses and farms, all providing work. The rector, Canon Hugh Price, was much loved and the policeman, PC Randall, kept a close eye to ensure that law and order were maintained.

Nurse Randall lived in the Toll House, Church Lane. She and the doctor provided a good local medical service. If she was not at home she left a blackboard outside her house where anyone requiring her services could write their name and address.

The men liked to meet up for a chat and a warm up at the fire in Worrall's Forge, High Street. Hadley's, the butchers in Bridge Street, had their own slaughterhouse and delivered meat to the big houses and supplied the workers as well. John Smith made and delivered fresh bread daily from his Wellesbourne Road shop. Carter's haberdashery shop in Church Street kept the knitters supplied with wool. There were few cars and only the big houses had telephones which could be used to place their orders with the village shops. Most people used bicycles to get around the village.

## Conscription

National Service or conscription existed from 1939 until 1960. The National Service (Armed Forces) Act made all males between the ages of 18 and 41 liable to conscription. Those engaged in vital occupations were exempt as were others for medical reasons. The age limit was raised to 51 in 1942 and females were included for the first time.

## The Blackout

The Blackout came into force on 1st September 1939, two days before the outbreak of war. Everyone had to cover their windows at night with heavy Blackout curtains, cardboard or paint to prevent any light from escaping which might aid enemy aircraft during bombing raids. Tape across the windows stopped the glass shattering. Streetlights were switched off or dimmed.

Hours of Blackout were published in the local newspapers, e.g. January 1943 5.42 pm to 8.45 am. The general impression among special constables was that the residents responded very well to the lights out appeal.
The Blackout restrictions lasted for five years.

"HULLO!—NOTICE ANYTHING ABOUT THE RAILINGS?"

## Removal of iron railings

Before WWII, photographs of Church Street and High Street properties show a lattice of iron railings dividing houses from the streets. These railings, and similar ones all over the country, were removed and used as scrap metal for war defences from 1942. Steel and iron was in short supply and removing the railings helped people believe that the village was doing its bit to help the war effort. Anyone who objected to the removal of the railings was condemned as unpatriotic. The railings were never replaced. The school bell was also removed at this time.

## St Peter's Church

In October 1939 the Parish Vestry members authorised Canon Price to purchase stirrup pumps, shovels and galvanised helmets for the purpose of dealing with fire caused by air raid damage. Arrangements were made for fire watching at the church and to cover the windows and doors to prevent powerful draughts in the event of fire. The Parish Vestry members were; Mrs Barker, Mrs Price, Miss Shirt, Sir Walter Howard, R Taylor, R W Hemmings, R Maisey, T Andrews and Mr Twigger.

Canon Price was very interested in recording village history, as was evident in his notes found in the church. In June 1941, he sent the church registers, which dated from 1537, to the Warwick County Record Office for microfilming and safe deposit.

## Barford before WWII, an eyewitness account

Norman Gardiner was born in Yew Tree Cottage, Wellesbourne Road, Barford, in 1923 and lived there until he enlisted in 1942. After he died in 2005, a document was found in his house and presented to Barford Heritage Group. The text of this document, which follows, depicts life and living in Barford before WWII.

***Barford was a small village with a population in the 1930s between seven and eight hundred. The village was essentially the main crossroads of the A429 running north to south known as Bridge Street and Wellesbourne Road with Church Street/High Street at right angles running east with various side streets and lanes off both roads.***

Bridge Street

***At the junction there was, and still is, an ancient giant cedar tree with most of the village shops grouped around. There are two pubs in the village the Joseph Arch and  the Granville Arms both on the A429. The Joseph Arch changed its name in the 1950s from the Red Lion to honour Joseph who was a village resident (and school pal of my grandfather) and founder of the Agricultural Workers Union in the late 1800s. The Granville Arms was managed in the 1950s and 1960s by Violet Short (née Winston) my step-sister Agnes' cousin. Joseph Arch's cottage can still be found opposite the church.***

*In the 1930s, the Red Lion was a Flowers ale pub, the brewery being situated in Stratford upon Avon and The Granville was an Ansells pub, Ansells being a Birmingham brewery and there was always a great rivalry between them.*

*St Peter's Church had, at this time, Canon Hugh Price as Rector. The village had a Church of England Elementary school, a Methodist Church, two garages, two butcher's (one was owned by the Hadley family who raised and slaughtered cattle, sheep and pigs locally), three grocer's and general stores (one was the paper shop), an excellent bakery and baker's shop, a bank, post office, timber yard, laundry and an indoor rifle range. This was also used as a village hall until the Smith-Ryland Memorial Hall was built in the early 1930s. One of the grocer's/general stores, owned by Freddy Lane, was also the local bookie – gambling shops were still illegal at this time so all off course betting was done under the counter. My mother liked a flutter on the horses and, as a boy, I was frequently sent to Freddy Lane's with a slip of paper and a couple of shillings to be handed over discreetly when no one was looking.*

*Mum each year received a book of Irish Sweepstake tickets for the Grand National in aid of the hospitals and she received one free ticket if she sold the rest of the book. One year in the mid-1930s she sold the winning ticket to the butler at Barford Hill House. He won £15,000, an absolute fortune in those days. He promptly retired, had a detached house built on the main road into Warwick, bought a new, large Armstrong-Sidley saloon car and became a toff himself. Barford also had a blacksmith's, owned by the Worralls, which was always busy shoeing horses (both carthorses and hunters), repairing implements, undertaking wrought-iron work and making tools. As children we always stopped by to watch and see the forge with its noisy bellows. The smell of burning hoof is something that remained with me for the rest of my life.*

*Young George Worrall and his father were great local characters and always ready to chat and explain what they were doing. At this time, every town and village had its own gas works to provide gas for cooking and originally for lighting (both homes and streets). Barford Gas Works was the last brick building on the edge of the village on the Wellesbourne Road near where my great-grandfather lived. The works closed down in about 1930 when new cast-iron pipes (about 4-5 inches diameter) were laid through the village from Warwick, an operation that took a very long time. As boys we took serious interest in its progress and most evenings sat around an oil-drum fire outside the night watchman's hut.*

Shows site of the old gas works

*He used to tell us blood-curdling stories about his experiences in the First World War. When the old Gas Works were demolished, we all assembled in my grandfather's field, 'Tritton's Field', to watch the felling of the big chimney into the corner of the field. We dispersed very rapidly as a huge cloud of soot and dust moved menacingly close.*

*One of my mates was Graham 'Bunny' Sutton who was the other village butcher's son. His grandfather was the local coffin-maker and undertaker and we often watched him at work building traditional wooden coffins, bending the side panels into shape and scorching the inside with burning wood shavings.*

*The main road through Barford was already fairly busy with traffic and before the 30mph limit was introduced, vehicles sped through the village and caused frequent accidents. One big hazard was the telegraph poles. In most places these were placed on the grass verges on the roadside. The lines were all above ground in those days and some of the poles were very large to carry the weight. As the road became busier, it was widened and straightened and the poles ended up very close to the edge of the road, most of them bearing scars from the numerous vehicles that collided with them. There was one such pole, just outside our wooden gate at Yew Tree Cottage, which was hit on several occasions. One night in the 1930s, after we (the children) had gone to bed, we heard a commotion downstairs and crept down to investigate. The house was full of injured people with blood and bandages everywhere. We were quickly ushered upstairs and next morning we awoke to see a car wrapped around 'our' telegraph pole, which had almost been severed in two.*

*In the 1920s and 30s, Sunday observance was a must for most people. The majority of the villagers were Church of England and many had regular pews in the Parish Church. The congregations at matins and evensong were quite large particularly at Easter and Christmas. There was also usually a very good attendance at the Methodist Church in Church Street but I have no recollection of a Jewish or Catholic contingent in the village although they were certainly highly represented at Warwick School when I attended later in life.*

*Very few people worked on Saturday afternoons or Sundays, apart from farm workers and downstairs staff in the many large houses in the area. All this changed when World War II started and most factories went over to seven days a week, twenty four hours a day shift working. For many people, Sunday consisted of early Holy Communion in church at 7 or 8 am with Sunday School in the village school at 10 am. The older children then went to church at 11 am for matins which normally lasted for an hour including a half-hour sermon and was also attended by many of the villagers, some of who would return for evensong at 6.30 pm.*

*The large area (now fully developed with houses) between Wasperton Lane (also known as the Allotment Lane) and the back boundary wall of Barford House belonged to the church and was set out as allotments. Villagers paid a few shillings a year to the church as rent and the fertile soil produced vast quantities of fruit and vegetables. My father had one of these allotments. Most men who did not attend church on Sunday mornings were busy in the allotments until luncheon time and many would visit the pub on their way home. Sunday afternoons and evenings, everyone dressed in their 'Sunday best' – children had to wear them all day. If the weather was good, whole families would go for a walk together in the afternoons after the best meal of the week: Sunday*

*luncheon; traditionally something roasted i.e. beef, pork, lamb, chicken or rabbit. In the summertime, the Sunday afternoon walk would often be to the allotments to see what was growing or to visit friends or relatives. On Sundays, my father usually got up early, between 6.30 and 7 am, did a couple of hours in the garden or allotment and then went fishing in the River Avon from my grandfather's field. After my voice broke and the Church choir no longer required me, I often accompanied him on these fishing exploits.*

*At about noon we stopped fishing, called in on Grandad for half an hour or so and then went to the Granville Arms for a quick pint, returning home for 1pm usually late!*
*After Sunday lunch he always went to bed until approximately 5pm then got up, washed, put on his 'Sunday best', had tea and went to Church in the evening.*

*From about the age of 8 until my voice 'broke', I was in the church choir, which meant attending matins and evensong every Sunday and choir practice on Friday evenings. The church organ was operated from a hand-operated bellows system in a tiny cubicle on the side of the organ. I had eventually succeeded Tony Hadley as head choirboy when his voice 'broke' and it was traditional for the retiring head to take over the task of pumping the organ so I, in turn, inherited that job for about a year. Inside the cubicle, a small pulley was let into the oak panelling on which was a cord, which had a brass weight on its end. Alongside the pump handle there were two lines on the panelling which you had to keep the brass weight floating between when pumping. You had to anticipate the start of each hymn to make sure the organ would operate, as there was always a steady leak from the system. Sleeping during the sermon was a serious hazard. Much time (and skill!) was spent in seeing how near the line you could leave it before the notes started to falter as the organist (a Mr Sturgeon – who was also the choirmaster) got very cross indeed when this happened – to the delight of the rest of the choir who were well aware of what had happened and why!*

*Playing 'out' with the lads was not permitted on Sundays and bike riding was only allowed if you were going somewhere specific. As a teenager, several of us usually went for a long walk on Sunday afternoons (Bob and Denis Taylor, Eric Watson and I) usually two or three miles maybe up Wasperton Lane, across the fields at Plestowes and back down past Hareway Farm to the cricket field. Other walks were to Wasperton and back or Longbridge along the Stratford Road and through Sherbourne.*

*We did a lot of bird nesting in the spring but tree climbing was out as we were in our Sunday best.*

*Every year there was a Summer Fete in the village and a fruit and vegetable show for which the competition was considerable. The Fete was held in the gardens of one of the big houses in the village in mid-summer and was always well attended. The earliest I remember was in about 1928 at Barford Hill. Mr Smith-Ryland (the village 'squire') had been in the Coldstream Guards and he arranged for the Guards Band to attend. I had never seen or heard a live band before and I remember the experience very well.*

*Other Fetes I remember were at 'Avonside' where I remember watching the dancing on the 'hard' tennis courts and again a military band playing behind the netting in the next tennis court. I was impressed with the ladies dressed in their finery of long dresses. Another Fete was held on the lawns of Barford House opposite Yew Tree Cottage and we had an excellent view of all the evening activities from our bedroom window.*

*We did a lot of swimming in the River Avon mainly above the bridge in Taylor's Orchard or at the 'River Banks' towards Wasperton. In the 1930s there was a bathing hut on the bank of the Avon on the first bend – about one hundred yards downstream of Barford Bridge. This hut was finally abandoned in the early 1930s when a young teenage girl called Watson (who lived in Church Lane) was drowned when swimming there.*

*The nearest cinema was at Warwick (the 'County') at the bottom of Smith Street. The first film I ever saw there was in about 1932 – it was called 'Thark' and was a comedy with several well-known stars of the time including Ralph Lynn and Gordon James. During the 1930s, my Dad and I often went to the County cinema on Saturday nights (their first house) either by bus or on our bikes during the summer.*

*The Whist Drive and Dance was a regular feature of the village in the 1920s and 30s. You paid separately for Whist or Dance or at a discounted price for both.*

*Whist was played (24 hands) from 7.30 pm to 10 pm followed by dancing to a live band from 10 pm until 1 or 2 am.*

*These events were usually held in the village hall and my parents frequently attended, as did I from the age of about 14.*

*There were also annual concerts – we all took part in these and I usually did as part of the Boy Scout or Cubs contribution.*
*Lantern Lectures were popular (there was no television in these days of course). Lectures were usually from Church Missionaries and were based around black and white slides. The subjects were normally life in wildest Africa.*

*Every year, the Warwickshire Yeomanry held their big summer camp in Warwick Castle Park (between the Castle and the Asps) on the Banbury Road and we always went to their open days. These were the days before they were 'mechanised' so they were all on horseback and hundreds of horses paraded and demonstrated their skills. The manoeuvres they took part in during their time at camp were often around the Barford area during our school summer holidays so we spent much time following them about on our bikes.*

*Bike riding was one of my favourite pastimes and Bob Taylor and I cycled every inch of the countryside for a 15-mile radius around Barford. At one time Bob's father was working as caretaker of several large huts full of railway and quarrying equipment at Edge Hill belonging to the then discontinued and mothballed Edge Hill Light Railway Company and their iron-stone quarrying operations. These operations were restarted during World War II. There were light engines and lots of rolling stock there and we used to cycle there and often picnicked amongst the steam engines (a twenty-five mile round trip).*
*The Barford village Football Club had been defunct for some years but was restarted in the late 1930s. They played on a very sloping pitch in the same field as the cricket pitch at Barford Hill on Plestowes Lane (Hareway Lane).*

*There was a very active Crown Green Bowling Club in a garden behind the Post Office in Bridge Street where my (by then one-armed) grandfather played. We still have his woods.*

*The Cricket Club was very active with a good square at Barford Hill and quite a large cricket pavilion where the teams enjoyed their sandwiches and homemade cake teas made and served by the cricket wives and supporters. Mary's husband, Jack Barlow (who lived at Hareway Farm only one field away), was an excellent wicket keeper and batsman. He played for the team for many years, becoming Captain and later Club Umpire, and was, for many years, Club President. Their boys, John and Ron, also played for the team for many years and later for Ashorne Club. I was never much good at cricket but acted as scorer for them when I left school and also as a 'make-weight' reserve when they were desperate. Prior to leaving school, of course, I had compulsory games on Saturdays at school so I was not available for village cricket.*

*Other organisations in the village flourished in the 1920s and 30s, notably the Women's Institute and the Mother's Union (who tended to be in competition with each other) and the British Legion. They all ran regular evening functions, particularly whist drives and dances.*

*The 1930s were the age of the Flying Circus and Air Display run by well-known personalities such as Alan Cobham, CWA Scott, Captain Black and others.*

*There was at least one display every year at Tachbrook Aerodrome which we always attended. I also remember two that were held at Barford in the meadow just upstream from Barford Bridge. One was by CWA Scott and was held on 18th September 1936 involving twenty aeroplanes. I also remember seeing the Airship 'R101' flying over the village at about this time.*

# Start of WWII – Home Guard

Anthony Eden, Secretary of State for War and conservative MP for Leamington and Warwick, (1923-1957) announced the formation of the Local Defence Volunteers or 'Home Guard' on the 14th May 1940. Barford was very quick off the mark.

Recruiting commenced at Barford Police Station on Sunday 26th May 1940. About thirty men signed up. Members were required to do a total duty of forty-eight hours in four weeks. Failure to attend resulted in a penalty of £10 or a month in prison. The patrols worked in pairs with two hours on and four hours off, two shifts per man. Training took place each evening and every Sunday morning and often lasted all day.

The assembly point was the old Rifle Range hut, down by Barford Bridge. The headquarters was a garage and a garden hut. It was equipped with electricity, telephone and a Primus stove to make tea. Two old mattresses were provided for those not on patrols. The toilet was a thick hedge at the bottom of the garden!!

Rifle Club top right

Ian Webster and his sister Sheila Reynolds remember the old Rifle Range and its surroundings as it was during the 1940s:

*The Rifle Range was beyond the current fishermen's car park and Phil Hammond's Yard. This was where all the joinery was done for the Smith-Ryland Estate. Our mother Flo was often given a handout of lime-wash to freshen up a room. We remember the Rifle Range being used as a rifle club and a youth club but have special memories of it being used on Coronation Day (it being typically English weather) as the venue for the Mill Lane and Bridge Street party.*

As winter approached the Home Guard section took over the ground floor room of the Working Men's Club, in what is now Cedar House.

Barford villagers enjoy a day out

A pillbox observation box was sited at Barford Bridge, as all roads were required to have observation posts. Chicanes of old railway sleepers were slotted into slanting concrete holes in the flood meadows and an old navy six-pounder gun was installed at one end of the bridge, opposite the observation box, and manned by the Home Guard.

6 pounder anti-tank gun

Norman Gardiner was the youngest recruit to the Barford Home Guard when he signed up on Sunday May 26th 1940.

Norman Gardiner 1942

Norman in Podva
Italy 1946

Norman Gardiner remembers:

***The following Sunday we assembled at the old Rifle Range hut, down by Barford Bridge. George Butler had been put in charge and the new 'Barford Platoon' consisted of a mixture of older men, most of whom had served in World War I, farmers and farm workers, exempted from Active Service, exempt factory workers; and two teenagers – Bill Freeman and me. At that first assembly we paraded with shotguns, air-rifles, broomsticks and the like. Several of the World War I veterans had been NCOs or officers including at least one ex-guards sergeant major, Harry Abbott, who attempted a bit of drill. Unfortunately in the 1930s the army had changed all their drills and organisation of units of fours to threes. This caused considerable confusion for the people who had served in World War I. As we had a Combined Cadet Corps at Warwick School, I was familiar with the new drill but naturally there was considerable reluctance to take any notice of the youngest member of the squad.***

*Nevertheless, it was not long before I was promoted to lance corporal and became a shooting instructor and grenade instructor. I think this was largely due to the support of our next-door neighbour, Harry Moore, who was a drill sergeant in the Royal Warwickshire Regiment at Budbrook Barracks. Barford Home Guard came under their wing and he was our training officer. Harry Moore joined the Royal Warwickshire Regiment as a boy soldier. He served in India for twelve years without home leave. He became an expert rifleman, representing his regiment in competitions. He lived with his family in 'Ypres Cottage' on the Wellesbourne Road.*

Harry Moore

*Our section consisted of Victor Cartwright (sergeant in charge), Jack Barlow (Mary's husband), Ken Upstone (Jack's farmer neighbour), Sam Shepperd (farm worker), Stan Udell, Killigan (ex-butler at Barford Hill but now a factory worker), Billy Bacon (village painter and decorator and comedian), and myself (now promoted to lance corporal and second in charge). Billy Bacon was probably over the age limit and reputedly lied about his age. He later became our first aid man, our 'Godfrey' of the TV series Dad's Army.*

*Victor Cartwright, a cavalry officer in World War I, now married to Mr Smith-Ryland's widow, Leila, and living at Barford Hill, got rather bored with things if there was no air activity by about 2 am. He would turn to me and say "If anything happens, you know my telephone number", then got on his bike and went home leaving me in charge.*

*At 7 am we rode back to Barford, opened the policeman's front door (a key was hidden in the garage – high security!), crept in and left our rifles.*

*I remember being 'captured' on several occasions, once by the army when I was taken away in an armored car and was interrogated properly – quite a frightening experience. On another occasion, I was captured on the top of Whitchurch Church tower as we were advancing to attack Leamington. I was taken away to the Lockheed factory and held in the canteen where I was given an excellent lunch.*

*We once attacked the Royal Air Force base at Wellesbourne Airfield by driving through the main gates hidden in the back of one of Oldhams' cattle trucks all baaing like sheep. To our surprise, the Royal Air Force regiment guards let us and the truck through!*

*Mr E G Oldham, who owned the main garage and petrol station in Barford, lived in Forge Cottage alongside the Wellesbourne Road (and river) some half a mile out of the village. On one dark night, one of his cars was jacked up on blocks and left on the grass verge outside his cottage. When Sam and I marched along the road, suddenly, in the distance, we heard the loud noise of a revving engine and found the car full of airmen who had decided to 'borrow' it to save walking the last two miles back to their base. In the darkness (and with brains fogged with alcohol) they had managed to start the engine but failed to see that the car had no wheels.*

*On another dark night, along the same stretch of road, we heard a commotion ahead. We found a party of drunken airmen, who had moved off the road to avoid a passing vehicle and as a consequence had fallen over a large lorry-load of stone road chippings dumped on the grass verge, scrabbling around in the bottom of the very muddy ditch unable to extricate themselves. Eventually, we got them out and then escorted them to Thelsford Bridge and off our territory. We did not always work amicably with the village policeman and his 'specials'.*

*One evening he brought us the message that a Czech deserter had escaped from the guardroom of the HQ of the Free Czechoslovakian Army at Moreton Paddox (about four miles away) and was reported to be heading our way. If caught, he was to be detained and the description was of a five foot eight inch tall, thickset, dark-haired, moustached man wearing battle dress and forage cap with Czech badges and other insignia. We were told also that he spoke no English.*

Station House Church Street

*In the early hours of the morning, Sam and I were coming over Barford Bridge when we saw a figure in the hedge bottom by the bridge wall. We issued the standard challenges: 'Halt – who goes there?' and 'Advance and be recognized!' with no reply. We fixed bayonets and advanced ourselves and pulled a very wet and muddy character out of the ditch.*

*He was bareheaded and wearing battle dress with the shoulder badges and insignia obviously and roughly torn off. He fitted the description of the deserter and as he appeared not to speak or understand English, we marched him to our HQ at the Working Men's Club in Barford and rang the police station.*

*A rather sleepy PC answered and I gave him the details. After a pause he replied.*
*"Is he wearing Czech badges?" –"No."*
*"Is he wearing a forage cap?" – "No" I replied.*
*"Then it can't be him – let him go."*
*I refused and we marched him down to the police station.*
*"He's all yours," we said.*
*He was promptly let free by the PC and we heard later that the Wellesbourne Platoon picked him up several hours later and it was indeed the wanted man.*

*The PC was not happy to be reminded about this story when I related it to him.*

Davinia Chambers remembers her mother Ada's encounter with the Home Guard:

***Well, it was the morning after the Coventry raid (Monday) and Monday morning as far as my mother's life was concerned was washday. Didn't matter if it rained, hailed – Monday was washday. Mr and Mrs Cheshire lived opposite and Mr Cheshire worked at the Dunlop. He used to cycle every day from Barford to Coventry so they were always up early, filling the coppers to get the water. Then my mother lit the fire and was about to go across the yard to do something, and she spotted this face creeping over Sir Walter Howard's wall and the face was followed by a body that slithered down to a heap and he crept up our yard! My mother was convinced that he was a German from a plane that had crashed overnight. Apparently all night long all they could hear was the Home Guards' whistles blowing where they were running up and down the village. My mother got the copper stick and hit this poor man on the back of the head and knocked him out. She ran down the village looking for Mr Workman and Mr Udell and all the other members of the Home Guard, and my mother thought as she was running down, "Golly, have I got enough clothing coupons left, because I'm bound to go and see the King because he'll thank me for killing a German!" She found the Home Guard and Mr Workman and a crowd of people came up and Mr Workman turned this man over, and said "For Christ's sake Ada, what have you done? This is the man from Coventry's Home Guard; they're out here, with a battalion, to help us."***

***But the end result was my mother never went to the palace but she went to the Home Guards' supper every year!***

Vic Cheshire remembers that:
***A volley of three rounds of rifle ammunition was fired at a rabbit, but missed. This was a serious misuse of ammunition and resulted in a full enquiry being held.***

However there was a very serious purpose for the activities of the Barford Home Guard.

The Home Guard watched for German parachutists as a major German invasion was expected. All open fields, especially the meadows, like those at Barford, were dotted with vertical poles and old railway sleepers to stop the landing of gliders.

Those fears were not unfounded in Barford as Mary Barlow recalls in her reminiscence:

***When bombing raids were in progress, Jack, myself and Jack's father, Tommy, often used to walk around the farm buildings checking for any incendiary bombs jettisoned by the raiders on their way home to lighten their load. Several fell very close to the rick yard at Hareway but we managed to extinguish most before they fully ignited. I had a complete bomb in my collection which had failed to ignite. During this period, farm tractors were not very common and all farms had carthorses. There was one old mare at Hareway called Kit who used to follow us around the fields during our inspection tours and each time we stopped, a soft nose would nuzzle over your shoulder and stay there until you moved off again.***

It was reported in the Leamington Spa Courier in June 1940:

***Mrs Ada C Wall, aged 34, Keytes Lane was injured by a bullet from the rifle of a soldier lately arrived from Dunkirk. She was admitted to the Warneford Hospital as the bullet had passed through her hand and into her body. The missile was removed at once and her condition became fairly comfortable.***

Reportedly, the incident occurred due to a dispute over a roll of toilet paper!

## The Women's Institute – jam, socks, eggs and pies in abundance

Barford Women's Institute was very active in helping the war effort.

Afternoon meetings were held from October 1939 because of the Blackout. Members started at once to knit socks for the Red Cross. At Christmas 1939, twenty soldiers were invited from Walton Hall to the Christmas party. Lady Burton announced in November 1942 that the ladies had knitted four hundred garments. Wool was again distributed to volunteers in October 1944 to knit for the children of liberated Europe and by June 1945, one hundred and sixty four articles had been produced. Treasure bags were also made at this time for wounded soldiers.

Members' annual county subscription was reduced to £2. 2s. 0d. from £3. 3s. 6d. for the duration of the War. Seed potatoes were offered to members and Mr Warren gave a talk on 'Wartime Gardening'. Haricot beans were suggested as a good winter crop. In June 1941 seeds arrived from America, which were issued to members after a ballot.

The Government requested that as many eggs as possible be preserved for the winter. One hundred and seventy six eggs were sent to the Warneford Hospital.

There were numerous fundraising events such as the 'Social Afternoon' held at Wasperton House by kind permission of Mrs Burton in September 1940. Leamington Courier reported: ***Mrs Barker, who lives in Watchbury House, organised a rummage sale. Miss J Wilkinson was kept busy with her pony and trap. Among the prizewinners were Mrs Barlow, Mrs Inson Mrs Huckvale, Mrs Whitehead, and Mrs Butler. Mrs Wimbush won a prize for her cake, Mrs Faulks for her bag making, Miss Shimwell won a chicken and Miss Bacon won a prize for correctly guessing the weight of a cake.***

Despite the enormous amount of extra work the ladies continued to enjoy competitions such as a Christmas Tree competition in 1943, intelligence tests, dancing, community singing and bowls of flowers competitions.

The ladies did not respond so well to a request to wash the socks of the soldiers camped at Longbridge. However Mrs Howard took charge of this, volunteering her house for the working party and volunteers came forward!

In June 1943 a letter was received from a prisoner of war, Lieutenant J Watson, thanking Barford WI for the gift of five hundred cigarettes and expressing his admiration for the work the women were doing for the war effort.

The Malt House

The Warwickshire Federation of Women's Institutes were engaged in endeavouring to preserve as much stoned fruit as possible for the 'Nation's Larder' from July 1940. There was a bumper crop of plums that year, so much so that there was not enough sugar for the purpose and the Government requested that the fruit be preserved with Campden Solution.

There was a request published for 7lb stone jars for this purpose. The Barford supply was to be sent to Mrs Roberts, Castle Cottage, Kenilworth. The Shipston on Stour jars were to be collected by Mrs Burton of Wasperton House. It is an interesting question as to why Mrs Burton, who was very involved with Barford WI, was not allowed to collect Barford jars.

As always, Barford started to organise resources very early and very well.

The WI borrowed a cooker for jam preserving from the Midland Electric

Light Company in April 1940. Five members volunteered to run the scheme with Miss Shirt in charge. She was also Treasurer.

The Rifle Range, which had gas laid on, was chosen as suitable premises. Mrs Burton offered to lend £20 to pay for sugar. Two committee members were sent to jam making school in May.

By October 1940 Mrs Oldham's report to the WI stated that 934lb of jam and four hundred and eighty nine cans of fruit had been produced. This was another very successful enterprise.

Mrs Hemmings, Produce Guild Secretary, had excelled in her work weighing up all the sugar and dealing with the returned produce. She even made a profit of £1 from the sugar!

In October 1941 Miss Shirt reported that 580lb of jam had been made! In October 1942 Miss Shirt stated that, in addition to 88lb of jam, 68lb of chutney had been sold locally. In August 1942 members were asked to collect rosehips. Mrs Howard took the bags to the depot and was paid two shillings per stone.

Despite all this wonderful work the WI Food Office refused to allow Barford ladies a permit to purchase a pound of tea for their meetings.

By July 1943 another 350lb of gooseberry jam had been made and in September another 164lb of jam was declared first class!

David Hemmings writes of his admiration for the ladies of Barford Women's Institute:

***They made a major contribution to food supplies through their jam making and fruit canning activities. I well remember these ladies boiling great pans of jam outside the Mill House surrounded by millions of wasps!***

Another three ladies attended jam making school in Leamington, and the jam preservation centre went into production again. This continued after the War. By 1949, five thousand cans of fruit had been preserved.

Iris Barlow remembers the popularity of canning fruit and vegetables:

***The canning took place in a house along the Wellesbourne Road but some of the results could be dodgy, particularly if the tins were blown.***

Iris also remembers that bottling was another way of preserving fruit and vegetables:

***Runner beans were often salted. Hareway Farm had no fridge in the early days, and cream and other foodstuffs were kept in the dairy, with the meat safe.***

Ethel Inson, Bella Pearce, Mrs Barlow, Mary Hemmings, Beat Hemmings, Grace Faulks, Ellen Moore, Flo Gardiner, Miss Hill.

Following their success with jam making the Barford Women's Institute decided to join the pie scheme and started selling pies at the end of July 1942. Mr Smith, the village baker, made two hundred pies which Mrs Oldham and Mrs Joynes sold to agricultural workers in the field. This venture was so successful that in August 1943 Mrs Carter, who owned a shop, was put in charge of the pie scheme to put it on a good business footing.

Barford Women's Institute continued to help others all through the war years. In February 1945, there was a good response to the appeal for gifts for the people of Shoreditch. Also at this meeting Mrs Hoskins gave a talk on 'The Curing of Small Parts of a Pig' which was followed by refreshments and a charade, performed by Mrs Hemmings, Mrs Faulks, Mrs Pearce and Mrs Udell. Mrs Barlow was the hostess.

Mrs Carter started a branch of the Services Coupon Free Knitting Wool Scheme in 1941.

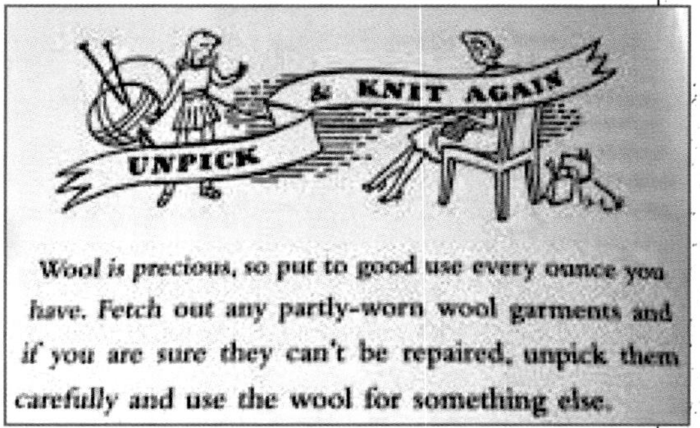

Barford Hill House

## The Spitfire Fund Fete

Extract from Leamington Spa Courier:

***Mrs Cartwright, in aid of the Spitfire Fund, organised a fete at Barford Hill. Over 400 people attended and £80 was raised. There was a tennis tournament. Miss Hodson, Seaford Ladies College, evacuated to Westham House, won the pig, in bowling for the pig. Mr Willis won the ducks. Mr Twigger, School Headmaster, was in charge of these events. Mrs J Smith-Ryland, Barford Hill, and Miss Emmet, formerly of Watchbury House, sold over 800 ices on a stall. Miss Pine ran the 'Post Office', Miss Willis the 'Hoop-la', Mr Forrest 'Hitting Coco-tins', Mr Cartwright and Charles Smith-Ryland, 'Aunt Sally', Mrs Tritton, Mr Ridgeway and Miss Pugh, Avonside House, also managed games. (September 1940)***

The Pugh family

## Baking for Barford and Coventry

Smiths Bakery, Wellesbourne Road

John Smith was born in Smallheath, Birmingham, but came to live and work in Barford in 1940. He bought the bakery business on the Wellesbourne Road from a Mr Freeman. He remembers:

***Unfortunately things were very, very scarce and we never made much money. The main thing was just making the bread and we had nothing in the shop so the wife used to close the shop at 1 o'clock and I'd make the bread and then for seventeen years she did all the deliveries to Sherbourne, Warwick and Barford. We had a little Morris van.***

***Tradespeople delivered to everyone in those days, except Mondays. I never did go to the War as such. I continued baking. Everything was very short during the War. Bread rationing continued until about 1954. We used to collect the coupons from the customers and make sure they were never short of bread.***
***Taking my memory back quite a little while, to the morning of Friday 14th November 1940, I got up at my usual time, about 3 am and started work. I called Tom Freeman about 5 am. Tom, who had previously owned the business, was still with us and helped me for a considerable time. As a rule he got up the same time as me. It was this Friday that the Germans decided to bomb Coventry. As we only lived twelve miles away we wondered if it was our turn next as we seemed to be in a direct run from their bombers.***

*We were lucky and escaped the bombing, but one bomber was brought down on the outskirts of Barford and poor Coventry got it very badly. We had only made sufficient bread for the day. We were just having a cup of tea in the bake house, about 5 am, when Lady Burton came to see us and asked if we could take some bread into Coventry.*

*The city was without bread and unable to make any because the water supply was completely shattered. She was disappointed that we hadn't any bread so I said to Tom, "Would you mind working with me through the night and make some?" So we set to, getting the oven going. At last we loaded up about 9 am and set off towards the outskirts of Coventry. We were stopped by police. "Where do you think you're going?" We had four hundred loaves and fifty gallons of water on board.*

*What a change when we told them we had water! The women were at their wits' end for clean water to make a cup of tea. They came over, hugged and kissed us and lifted us up and wept and they wouldn't let us unload the van, they said it was the least they could do and told us to sit back and have a rest. I realised how tired I was and that I had to drive home to Barford. I went fast asleep and did not wake up until the unloading was finished.*

## Women's Land Army/ land girls

Kathleen Davis of the Red House has a clear recollection of land girls working in the village and their effect on the village lads:

***And of course we had land girls, a bevy of land girls, going down to the pub and I'll tell you what, the village lads had never seen anything like it! One did marry a lad from Barford. She was a very good-looking girl!***

Actually at least two land girls married Barford boys!

Irene Wells describes the uniform of the Land Army:

***We put on our short sleeved, cream, aertex shirts and our green wool jumpers and then got into our breeches. There were hoots of laughter as we got into those feeling that they made us look twice our normal size. The breeches had three buttons on each side of the waist to fasten them and there were laces, which we had to fasten below the knee. On top of these we had a short topcoat and a hat, both a medium brown colour. We wore wool knee socks and heavy brown shoes. A badge in gold, red and green was also supplied. This had on it a sheaf of corn and there was a crown on the top of the badge. We later bought ourselves belts and green ties to finish the uniform off. There was a lot of laughing and joking as we dressed ourselves up that day and these clothes certainly felt odd at first but we soon began to feel at home in them.***

There were land girls billeted at Barford Hill, at Keytes Lane with Mr and Mrs Benfield, with William Canning at Debden Farm and with Jack Canning at Wasperton. Jack and Mary Barlow who farmed at Hareway Farm used to share Jack Canning's land girls when there was extra work to do.

Land girls worked at Carter's farm in the village. One of these girls, Ruby Colson, describes how after training she was first sent to Little Kineton, to work for a Mrs Fieldon. During her time there a horse ate her smalls washing! The American Garland family invited the girls to a party at Moreton Hall. (This family had lived at Watchbury, Barford, for a short time.) While at the Moreton Hall party, one of the girls, Sophie, met a Mexican, whom she later married and they moved to Mexico.

When Mr Fieldon died the house at Kineton was sold and Ruby moved to work with her friend Dora at Barford.

There was a constant stream of trucks carrying soldiers through the village of Barford. Ruby and Dora worked at muckspreading for Mr Carter, who had a milk round for a time. Mrs Carter was a marvellous cook and the girls were in heaven as the meals in Kineton had been frugal. Dora and Ruby both married during their stay in Barford. Dora left straight after her marriage but Ruby stayed on as her husband had to return to Austria where he was stationed. Day after day was spent pulling mangolds and by February Ruby had enough of this and also left.

Perhaps Ruby was one of the land girls who went carol singing and raised £3 for the Prisoner of War Fund. Perhaps Miss Christmas, who lodged with the Tallis family at Sherbourne Hill, was one of the singers. The Women's Institute invited the land girls to their monthly meeting in March 1942.

Another land girl who worked in Barford, at Canning's Farm in Debden Hollow, was Joan Christian. Joan grew up in a London suburb. During her training before coming to Barford she was billeted with a cowman, learning to care for cattle and to harvest sugar beet with frozen, icy tops.

She had to carry water up narrow stairs to have a bath and it was difficult carrying the full bath back down to empty it! After a time she was billeted at Debden Farm and had to share a bed with Ivy Poole, another land girl, even though they had not met before. They fed the stock, planted and harvested potatoes, and helped load the bags of potatoes onto the lorries taking them away. They also stacked corn and threw the sheaves upon the carts. If it was very wet they sat in the loft above the stables mending sacks. Another land girl, Doreen, was the only one allowed to thatch the ricks.

The land girls were invited to the dances in the village hall and met the troops stationed in Wellesbourne. There were few males in the village between the ages of 16 and 50. Some of the farm labourers resented the land girls as they thought that they had replaced the younger male workers, but in reality the young men had been called up and the farmers had no choice but to let them go.

For all their hard work the girls were paid £1. 7s. 6d. a week but had to pay £1. 0s. 0d. to the landlady for their board. They were given two free train tickets home a year but Warwickshire is a long way from Kent and Joan could not afford to go home more often.

After three years Joan returned to Kent but remained friends with Ivy, who stayed in Barford. Ivy married Jack Canning, the farmer's son.

**Molly Canning**

Molly Canning of Debden Farm was the country organiser for the Women's Land Army and helped to train the girls at Park Hall, Salford Priors. Molly's family had farmed around Barford and Wasperton for generations. She was well qualified to teach farming but she also had a Certificate in Home Nursing and First Aid from the British Red Cross. She attended many courses with the St John Ambulance Association and at the end of the war was presented with a certificate in recognition of devoted service to the cause of humanity by Queen Elizabeth, the President of the Society. Molly was presented to the Princess Royal, when she visited Ragley Hall in 1941 on a tour of inspection of Red Cross Hospitals. Molly had to make sure that the land girls were well fed, had a bike and were not overworked. Some farmers did not look forward to her visits!

Debden Farm

Parts of Barford Hill House were used to accommodate the land girls and they were under Molly Canning's control. She arrived each morning to give the girls their orders for the day and to inspect them, on parade, in their uniforms. She was very strict. Molly was allowed extra petrol coupons to carry out her duties.

Molly Canning being presented with her British Red Cross Medals.

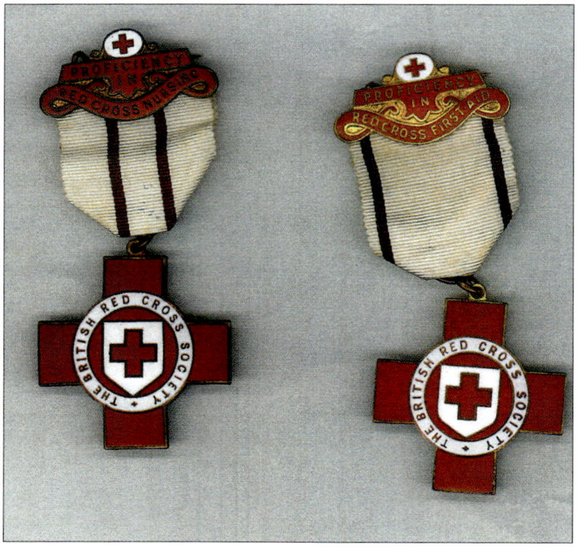

## German and Italian prisoners of war

There was a prisoner of war camp, which was used for German prisoners, at the Asps on the Banbury Road.

David Hemmings caught a German airman who had parachuted down near the river in the Westham House area. The only weapon this prisoner had was a pitchfork and he was expecting to be shot. David and the prisoner were both scared but David managed to take his prisoner to Warwick Police Station.

David Hemmings

Dick Cherry remembered working on Jack Canning's farm at Wasperton. He was there when a German plane crashed and Jack caught the pilot who was shouting "Comrade, comrade!" Three Germans parachuted out and if you go to Wasperton you will see that there is a branch still missing off a tree as one of the parachutes caught on the tree and broke the branch off. All three were captured. The Home Guard had a sandbag emplacement along the Wellesbourne Road, where the bus stop is, and the captives were held there until the army took them away.

Mary Winnington recalls: It was towards the end of the War that a German plane came down in the river at Wasperton. Arthur Workman, a special constable, accompanied by PC Randall, a rather large constable, went in his Austin 7 to investigate and found the pilot caught by his parachute in a tree. He was duly taken prisoner and driven in that very small car to Warwick Police Station, PC Randall sitting in the back, and the captive in the front.

Sonia Farley's mother had a pair of sandals, woven from straw, made for her by a German prisoner who was working in the village.

Baker John Smith, who had his bakery and shop on the Wellesbourne Road, had both Italian and German prisoners working for him He remembers:

***We had two Italian prisoners of war and neither of them were any good! They were subscripted to me and I was managing fairly well, but it was getting a bit heavy and the powers that be said I should have these two blokes. They came out every day. The prisoner of war camp was just by the road off the Banbury Road, at the infants' school, and Robert was stationed there and the wife used to go and pick him up every morning. He was German. Robert Waltz, was his name. He stayed until the end of the War, had breakfast with us, as his meat ration was minute.***

***He said "Mr Smith, tiles dirty on the roof. I'll take them off." He stripped the whole building. His original job in Germany was as a baker. Robert asked me if he could have some ingredients for a Christmas cake competition at his camp. I told him he could have what he wanted. He won the competition and that made his day. Unfortunately both he and I used to smoke a lot of cigarettes and I used to supply him. We both used to smoke about twenty a day.***

***On a Saturday, after I had been up all night working, he would come in. He used to wash the entire bakery from top to bottom; you couldn't have found a cleaner place. He enjoyed doing it.***

***When the War ended he stopped being an SS, and became quite human!! He was one of the family and we all loved him. He didn't want to go back to the Russian zone and he stayed in England. The only way he could stay was as an agricultural worker, a wicked waste. Robert worked on a farm in the area when in about 1948 my father crushed his hand, the farmer let Robert come back and run the bakery for us until his hand was better.***

***He met his wife to be whilst she was working in the Land Army. They were both German and took out British nationality. They lived in Kent. She died not long ago but Robert is still alive, must be in his eighties. Our children adored him.***

## Czech soldiers

'Camberleesh', 'Kataraboo', 'Lee Reich' – these were strange sounding names of Czech soldiers billeted in Barford in 1940! Vic Cheshire, Gerald Mason, Harold Tilling and Dick Cherry were among the villagers introduced to a whole new language and culture at an early age.

In late June and early July 1940, within a month of the evacuation of the British Expeditionary Force from Dunkirk, there was a withdrawal of several thousand Czechoslovak soldiers from the Continent; a large number of them arrived at Liverpool.

After a period of reorganisation in Cheshire over three thousand troops were moved to more comfortable quarters in Warwickshire in October 1940. The various units were dispersed to a number of requisitioned country houses to the south-west of Leamington, including a unit based in Barford.

The troops were housed in various houses in the village. Captain Barker, who lived in Watchbury House, was in charge of the Intelligence Corps. The Czech soldiers 22nd Liaison headquarters was at Barford Hill House, under the command of Colonel Pollock, assisted by Major Fillingham, Captain Hart and Captain Griggs.

Davinia Chambers remembers the Czech soldiers billeted in her home:

***We had Czech soldiers billeted on us. Mr Randall, who was the village policeman, had to suss out who was sleeping downstairs because he needed the accommodation for people displaced by the bombing raids on Coventry and Wellesbourne. We don't know whether his wife found this out at the WI meetings. He would come round and say "I understand you got two bedrooms empty upstairs, can you have x number of evacuees?" They had two of these Czech solders billeted at Watchbury House up Church Street.***

***One of them had been a builder in his life because he altered the fireplace at home, and the other one was a commercial artist and he made us Christmas trimmings and decorations out of split down margarine cartons, great big things, and for years as a child I thought Merry Xmas was a Czech way of spelling Christmas, because all this man had done was written Xmas on the decorations. I hadn't been to school then, I didn't know!***

Czech Memorial Fountain Jephson Gradens Leamington Spa

The Czech soldiers taught the village children to make faces at the German prisoners of war working in the village!

A Barford lady remembered that Czech soldiers billeted in Barford, one of whom was her boyfriend, were sent on a mission to assassinate Reinhard Heydrich, head of the combined security services of Nazi Germany.

The Czech soldiers are commemorated on a plaque by the fountain in the Jephson Gardens, Leamington Spa.

## Lady Duncanson and the Victoria League, overseas servicemen in Barford

Rear view of the Red House

Sir John and Lady Duncanson took up residence in the Red House at the start of the War. In 1943, Sir John was made controller of British Iron and Steel which had its headquarters at Ashorne Hall. In the same year he undertook a world tour as a member of the Anglo-American mission to survey steel production and use. He travelled fifty thousand miles in ninety three days, visiting New Zealand, Australia, the Middle East, South Africa, Rhodesia and Canada. He continued in this post until 1948 when the family left Barford to return to Scotland.

Sir John does not appear to have taken an active part in village life but Lady Duncanson did. Their daughter, Anne, attended Seaforth Ladies College, Sussex, which was evacuated to Westham House for the duration of the War. The Red House had tennis courts and Charles Smith-Ryland used to come to play with their son, Tom, who attended Warwick School. The tennis courts were used by the Duncanson's friends and not by the village generally.

Westham House

Lady Duncanson was a member of the Victoria League, an organisation founded in 1910 to promote friendship and understanding among people of the Commonwealth.

Kathleen Davis worked at the Red House for the Duncanson's. She worked as a cook, replacing a lady who was forever getting drunk because she was badly affected when her husband was killed when a bomb hit the Lockheed factory.

Kathleen Davis

Mrs Abbott came in to do the laundry. Kathleen remembers visits by numerous 'Government people' for dinner, and also visits by people from the Iron and Steel company in a big black car with parcels of food, some of which Kathleen divided up among the other staff.

Commonwealth servicemen were frequent visitors to the house through Lady Duncanson's involvement with the Victoria League.

Kathleen Davis remembers:

***Lady Duncanson belonged to what was called the Victoria League. A Lady Reading started it and it was to give a weekend break or a week's holiday for our troops from Canada, New Zealand and Australia, the entire Commonwealth. So we'd have a phone call and it would say, "Can you take two New Zealand aircrew?" She would say to me "Kathleen get your skates on, we are going to Elizabeth's at the top of the Parade." Lady Duncanson queued with everyone else, to get whatever we could to help with food because things were difficult and of course we had a bit of black market stuff. I was given £5 and told to go over to a farm called Boswells at Sherbourne, no names or pack drill! They just put things in a bag and I came back with it.***

***We had two Canadians, flying crew. One was a member of the equivalent of our SAS; he'd been on the Nijmegen Bridge and killed two Germans. He had cut their Iron Crosses off them. There were two and I had one. Rosemary stole it. Never had it back, no.***

***When we queued up at the Parade, we got steak and kidney pies, because we had difficulty with food, and some sort of cakes.***

***We put the Canadians up for three or four days, they might have a weekend or might be a week, and when the War was over Sir John and Lady Duncanson went to each of these boy's countries to meet the parents of those who got back. They sent me chocolate for the wee chappy because we couldn't get any.***

Kathleen Davis worked for the Duncansons until she had to leave when she became pregnant with her son in 1945. Her husband worked elsewhere and he stayed away during the week. Kathleen went to live in one of the three old thatched cottages where Barley Close, High Street is now.

She moved from the grand Queen Anne Red House to an unsanitary, rat-infested cottage. Kathleen was asked to go and work for Lady Duncanson in Scotland, with the promise of a job for her husband, but she decided to stay in Barford. She kept in contact with the family when they left the village and visited Lady Duncanson when she lived at Hove, taking her out for picnics.

Kathleen Davis, Mary Winnington, Gerard Mason and Davinia Chambers have vivid memories of Canadians and American servicemen visiting Barford.

Gerard remembers: ***When convoys of American soldiers went through the village, the children would call "Got any gum, chum?" and would run and pick it up as they threw it to us. The village came through the war unscathed, which was fortunate considering the close proximity of airfields at Wellesbourne and Longbridge where still the skeleton of a hanger remains.***

Davinia says: ***When my uncle came home on leave, we always had a yellow telegram – "Meet me off the bus, arriving Barford."***

***And this one from my uncle George said, "Arriving Barford with two friends for the weekend." So our Michael and me were sent down to the bus stop and my Uncle got off the bus and he'd got two black men with him. We had never seen a black man before and this one black man had a gold tooth.***

***I was convinced he was a prince. They were Jamaicans.***

***In the evening there was a dance in the village and these two black men could do the jitterbug so the Barford girls thought it was wonderful.***

***On the Sunday morning our Michael and me were sent upstairs to take them a cup of tea, because they used to come home purely for a rest. My mother used to get the copper and they had a bath. When we opened the bedroom door I was absolutely mortified, they were still black! I looked at the sheet to see if it was black, but no. They were still as black in the morning as they were the night before.***

***The village girls were on our pump waiting to see these chaps.***

Kathleen remembers: ***Wellesbourne airfield was operational. As you came from Charlecote under that main crossroad to Loxley, there was a Wellington bomber always there. They were flying over at night and I do think a German plane crashed in Wasperton. Somebody said you could still see the ghost. The plane dropped in a tree. We saw a piece of it when we used to go fishing; somebody dug it up, didn't they? The dances were full of Canadians, jitterbugging and everything. I'll tell you what, the drains got so full up that they wanted someone to come up and clear it – it was full of you know what's! So I was told. There was this six foot tall Canadian and every time he got too far drunk he'd got to give a speech. They were forever getting him off the stage.***

Mary remembers: ***Maud Workman would often bake cakes for the convoys of American soldiers who passed along Wellesbourne Road. They were gladly received and Mary would be lifted onto the lorries and from metal trays would hand them out to the troops.***

Maud Workman at the gate of the second cottage Westham Lane

Arthur & Maud Workman on their Golden Wedding

Wellesbourne Mountford Airfield was devoted to the training of UK and Commonwealth aircrews: pilots, navigators, bomb aimers, wireless operators and air gunners, mostly Canadians. Wellesbourne lost ninety-six Wellingtons on operations and training accidents; eighty airmen were killed and three hundred and fifteen injured. Some men who took part in the famous Dam Buster raid trained there.

On August 25th 1942 a Wellington bomber, based at Wellesbourne Airfield, was returning from a training exercise at night when it crashed into the bank of the River Avon in Wasperton parish killing all five of its Canadian crew.

On July 23rd 1943 a Whitley bomber, based at Long Marston, crashed into Scar Bank, the steep cliff close to the crash site of the Wellington but on the opposite side of the river, in the parish of Hampton Lucy. The aircraft was on a night practice bombing mission to Idlicote bombing range near Shipston-on-Stour and was returning to base. All five members of the crew, consisting of four from the Royal Air Force, along with the Australian pilot, lost their lives. Blazing trees on Scar Bank could be seen from Wasperton and Barford. Two large and two light fire pumps, a mobile dam and a foam tender took a long time to reach the site due to difficult access on to the bank. Pontoons were used to transfer the wreckage from Scar Bank across the Avon.

In the late 1970s the Stratford Aviation and Militaria Enthusiasts erected an unusual memorial consisting of two propeller blades on the river bank. It was dedicated in April 1977. A plaque naming the crew members of both planes has been erected.

The memorial has been registered with the National Inventory of War Memorials.

Further information can be found in the Air Museum at Wellesbourne Airfield.

One American soldier, George Sevy, was based at Wellesbourne during the War. George explains why he came here to use his skills as an aircraft engineer:

***I was raised to believe all people are equal and when Hitler kept sending troops into other European countries for occupation, England and her Allies were not strong enough to defeat the German axis, so I came to help the Allies and joined the United States Army Corps, hence my presence in England for over three years. War is never a good idea, but World War II proved that good does triumph over evil.***

Whitley bomber

Ivy Canning at Scar Bank Wasperton

## Toc H

Reverend Phillip Byard Clayton founded Toc H in France in December 1915 to provide a rest house for the troops. The original name, Talbot House, was shortened to Toc H by the troops.

The first hostel opened in London in 1919 as a home for men coming to London for work and having nowhere to stay. When the men returned home they set up groups of Toc H to carry out this service in their home areas.

The organisation grew rapidly in the 1930s, so much so in Warwickshire that it was necessary to divide the county into two parts, each with a district committee. Barford was under the guidance of the group headquarters in Leamington.

Rev Clayton visited the area in 1934. During the years of WWII Barford Toc H members who were not in the services joined the Home Guard and the British Legion.

After the War the branch, which met in the Memorial Hall, was used as a meeting place for ex-servicemen.

This photograph below shows members attending a service with other local branches.

Barford Toc H

***Front row:*** *Dick Hemmings, F Bacon, L Bister, Ed Hadley*
***Back row:*** *Jack Barlow, Phil Hammond, Roy Maisey, George Worrall*

No. 77.

BRITISH LEGION
(Early 1930's.)

BACK ROW

1. Mr. Harris Wasperton
2. ?
3. Mr. Smith Wasperton
4. Mr.P.Castle
5. ?
6. Mr.F.Andrews
7. Mr. F.Whitehead
8. Mr. T. Andrews

MIDDLE ROW

1. ?
2. Mr.Bertie Smith
3. ? Mr. Geens
4. Mr.J.Price
5. Mr.J.Wiltshire
6. Mr.C.Pitcher
7. Mr.Gardner
8. Mr.Harryfield
9. Mr.J.Booker
10. Mr.B.Winston

FRONT ROW

1. Mr.J.Pearce, 2. Mr.Byerley, 3. Mr.J.Harrison, 4. Mr.A.Rothbottom, 5. Mr.D.May, 6. Sir.W.Howard, 7. Major B.Tritton, 8. Mr.L.Bass, 9. Capt.Farley, 10. Mr.Miller-Smith, 12. Mr.R.Hemmings

11.not known

## Barford branch of the British Legion

The Legion organised whist drives and dances to raise funds and keep spirits up during the war years. The British Legion was founded in 1921 to provide financial, social and emotional support to those who had served in the armed forces and their dependants. Earl Haig was a founder member of the Legion and President, until his death in 1928.

At the Armistice Day Service in St Peter's Church, in November 1939, fifteen Legion members were present. By October 1941 the membership had risen to forty. At this time Mr C Pitcher was President and Mr H Field was Secretary. At the remembrance service Mr T Hewitt, an ex-service man, placed the Legion wreath at the memorial.

Major Tritton was President in November 1942. A British Legion dance held in the Memorial Hall in December of that year was so successful that a number of people had to be turned away. The Leamington Courier reports: ***Over one hundred people attended. The Jonquils Dance Band supplied the music. Mrs Barlow and her partner won a novelty dance competition. Mr Pitcher was Master of Ceremonies and the branch benefited by £6.***

***There was a large attendance at the whist drive in September 1943. The lucky ticket, for a basket of grapes donated by Mrs Barker of Watchbury House, went to Margaret Carter and was presented by June Smith-Ryland. There were many other winners including H Tilling, F Bidwell, R Taylor, Mrs Cheshire, Miss Hill, Mrs Davies, Mrs Freeman and M Harvey. Mrs Joynes was in charge of refreshments.***

At another dance in 1943 the Bartonian Orchestra supplied the music.

***Members of the Legion, Home Guard, Observer Corps, Air Raid Protection Services, Women's Section of the Legion, Girl Guides, Wolf Cubs and pupils from Seaford Ladies College, Westham, attended the Armistice Day Service in November 1943. There was a parade from the Red Lion (now the Joseph Arch pub) to the church. Brigadier General Baylay, Barford House, inspected the services assembled.***

There was a very active women's section of the Legion in the village. They organised many whist drives; games, such as musical parcels; and darts competitions, in the Memorial Hall. Usually about fifty people attended these events.

In May 1943, the committee of the Women's Branch served refreshments at a party in the Memorial Hall to celebrate the 16th birthday of Master Charles Smith-Ryland. The hall was decorated with flags and flowers. Over one hundred guests each received a piece of the birthday cake. The Serenade Band played for dancing and a collection was taken for the Royal Navy.

Barford British Legion was mentioned in the Leamington Spa Courier on 31st December 1943 for providing Christmas gifts for the patients at Warwick Hospital.

## Rationing

Food rationing was introduced on Monday 8th January 1940, during one of the coldest winters on record. Bacon, butter and sugar were first to be rationed and soon after meat, tea, jam, biscuits, breakfast cereals, cheese, eggs, milk, canned and dried fruit were added. Almost all controlled items were rationed by weight, but meat was rationed by price. Fresh vegetables and fruit were not rationed but some types of imported fruit, such as lemons and bananas, became unobtainable.

Bread came off ration in 1948 but sugar rationing did not end until September 1953 and meat rationing not until all food rationing ended on 4th July 1954.

Clothes rationing came into force in June 1941 and ended on 15th of March 1949. The allowance was the equivalent of one new outfit per year, so hemlines rose and double-breasted suits went out because of a lack of material. Sachets or bottles of 'liquid silk stocking' provided a substitute for real stockings, or gravy browning could be used with a pencil liner for the seam!

Petrol was rationed in the first year of the War and on 1st July 1942 the basic civilian ration was abolished. After that fuel was only available to emergency services, bus companies and farmers and of course armed forces. The basic petrol ration was restored on 1st June 1945.

The location of Barford, surrounded by rich farmland, and most of the village houses having gardens, meant Barford survived well during the years of rationing.

Those who were children in the village then remember that there was little shortage of Victoria sponge and of course the jam to fill it.

Barford Parish Council decided to plough up part of the playing field to plant corn, as requested by the Agricultural Committee, at a meeting in April 1940. In August 1941 the Parish Council held a meeting to decide what to do with the oats grown for the 'Dig for Victory' campaign. It was proposed to get S B Morton of Longbridge Farm to undertake the harvesting and to sell the grain on behalf of the Parish Council. The Parish Councillors were concerned about how to protect the crops.

Mr Hadley took over the playing field, at a rent of £5 per year, in September 1941. He continued to farm this land until September 1949.
Many residents had a share in a pig, which was a wonderful recycling machine, consuming the leftovers. Others kept a pig of their own but shared the meat with their friends and neighbours.

Vic Cheshire recalls: ***Mr Arty Wells used to kill the pigs. He arrived with his tools attached to his belt and there and then it was killed! After cleaning, the pig was hung on a beam in the scullery. The bits of the pig which could not be preserved were shared around with other families, secure in the knowledge that they too had a pig which would be shared out in turn.***

Joyce Perrott, then a small child, remembers, in graphic detail, how pigs helped to keep the village fed during the War:
***When a pig was killed, straw was set alight and used to burn off the bristles. Then the skin was scrubbed to remove the debris. Some of the villagers owned a pig bench, which I think was lead lined, with a hole for drainage. An incision was made down the front of the pig and all the organs removed. Liver was called 'fry' and tasted delicious, cooked straight from the pig. The pancreas was 'sweetbread', the heart was stuffed and cooked, kidneys were fried and the small intestine was cleaned and boiled and eaten cold with vinegar. These were called 'chitterlings'.***

***Brawn was made from the pig's head, which was boiled whole, and the meat from the cheeks, etc. removed, set in a mould and eaten cold. The fat from round the kidneys was suet, used in puddings, and the apron of fat covering the abdominal organs rendered down as lard, with the crunchy bits remaining eaten as scratchings. The tongue was cooked, pressed down with heavy weights and eaten cold. The stomach was cleaned and boiled as tripe and served with parsley sauce. Pigs' trotters were also boiled and considered a delicacy. I remember seeing 'lights' (lungs) hanging in the butcher's shop. I don't know if anyone ate them, certainly dogs did. Nothing was wasted. Some of the women in the village were expert in dealing with all of this but many thought it too messy!***

***Pig meat, eggs, vegetables, etc. were always shared around and when the womenfolk made cakes, jams, etc. they would invariably give some to the neighbours. There were some very poor families in the village, particularly farm workers living in tied cottages, and I remember children having to walk two or three miles to school in very inadequate clothing. The thought of their red chapped fingers and cold wet feet as they walked through the snow wearing plimsolls fills me with sadness even now.***

Eggs were an important part of the wartime diet; any family with even a small garden kept hens. Davinia Chambers remembers that each person was only allowed one and a half eggs per week and any left over had to be handed over to the egg marketing man who used to come in his red van on a Friday. Davinia also remembers a cunning tip from a lady evacuee:

***If you had some evacuees with you, if you had white eggs, you had so much and if you had brown eggs you had three farthings more a dozen. This one lady evacuee that came to stay with us, she used to reckon that if my mother were to tip the teapot into the bucket the eggs would all come out brown and my mother could have this other three farthings a dozen. It wasn't a lot of money but three farthings could probably buy two Oxo cubes or something.***

The weekly shopping trip to Stratford upon Avon or Warwick was a highlight for Barford ladies. Iris Barlow's mother-in-law used to cycle to Insons and then catch a bus to Stratford upon Avon, then repeat the journey, laden down with bags. The Co-op was a favoured shop for bacon, and a trip to Ferris's, a delicatessen, was a treat.

Tea was rationed and it was a cause for celebration when Davinia Chamber's uncle in Burma sent a 7lb crate of tea home. Davinia remembers:

***Mrs Griffin was the post lady then and she would be walking up the street and saying to everybody, "Oh, there's tea going to Ada's" and in the afternoon my mother's cronies would turn up with a piece of tissue paper and my mother gave them a scoop of tea. This particular afternoon when my mother's friends came round, there draped on the piano was a parachute and two black ebony elephants. My uncle hadn't sent tea, he'd sent presents! My mother made underwear and stuff out of parachute silk.***

New clothes required coupons. Kathleen Davis recalls Lady Duncanson having to spend some of hers:

***Sometimes the undertaker, can't think of his name, he lived somewhere along the main road, used to deliver the papers. Lady Duncanson's dog tore the behind out of his trousers and she didn't know what to do. I said "You'll have to give him another pair because they're couponed!"***

Lady Duncanson was fined £15 at Warwick Borough Petty Sessions in September 1943 for using petrol for a purpose other than that for which coupons were issued to her. A summons for wasting petrol was dismissed. Lady Duncanson had taken her children to Jephson Gardens to hear the band when she was apprehended. The Leamington Courier reported: ***She said that the buses from Barford to Leamington were always very full and it was impossible to say with any certainty if a passenger would be able to get on.***

Joseph Rouse, a singing bus driver who lived in Barford, was fined £2 for using his car on a Sunday. He was only allowed petrol to travel to his work in Leamington. This was in November 1943.

Edward Guy Oldham of Forge Cottage had three summonses against him dismissed in June 1942 and was awarded costs of £20 to be paid by the Ministry of Fuel and Power. He had permission to transport agricultural produce to Stratford upon Avon, Warwick and Leamington, and also permission to collect urgent spare parts from manufacturers for cattle transport vehicles. This was work of national importance and Mr Oldham's car was never used for pleasure.

Mrs Oldham did use the car for transporting canned produce but this was voluntary. Miss M E Rotherham, JP, said she did not know anyone who worked harder for the nation than Mrs Oldham. The WI shop in Leamington was dependent on the generosity of Mrs Oldham and her petrol to reopen. The court decided that the Oldhams should not be out of pocket for their voluntary work.

## School

During the years of the WWII Barford St Peter's School was an 'all age' school with pupils staying on until the end of their education.

Mr Arthur Spencer Twigger was appointed Headmaster in 1936 and remained in this position until he retired in the early 1960s. Mr Twigger, one of the three children of Albert and Mabel Twigger, was born in Warwick. He married Claire Ravenhall in 1932. They had two children, Pat and John, and the family lived in the schoolhouse beside the school. His pupils remember him with respect, even though some of them, including his own children, received strokes from his cane! The number of pupils during the war years was approximately one hundred.

Mrs Calvert was the assistant teacher. She taught four different age groups in one room; a total of thirty children. Just before Mothering Sunday Mrs Calvert went with her pupils into the woods to pick violets.
She then packed the flowers and sent them to London by train for the mothers of the evacuee children.

Joyce Perrott remembers some of the books the children learned to read from and the songs they learned to sing:

***Our books were old-fashioned and rather boring but were hard to come by in those days. For example, 'Nan rode in the gig'. We sang songs of 'Rickety Tick' and 'I wish, how I wish that I had a little house.'***

***'How I wish'***

***How I wish, how I wish that I had a little house,***
***With a mat for the cat and a holey for the mouse,***
***And a clock going 'tock' in the corner of the room,***
***And a kettle and a cupboard and a big birch broom.***

The poorest children wore Wellington boots to school, often without socks. All boys wore short trousers. The clothes the children wore were mostly made at home, often from garments handed down though the family.

The senior boys stoked the boiler in winter and placed their jacket potatoes on top to cook for break time. They carved their initials so they could tell who owned each potato. The children who lived in the village went home for lunch but the children who lived on the farms surrounding the village had to stay in school. Kind Mrs Claire Twigger and Mrs Foster organised the cooking of school dinners for these children. This was before the 1944 Education Act made it an entitlement for pupils to receive a free school meal.

Most of the children walked or cycled to school on their own. There were few cars on the roads then.

The impact of the War on Barford School was felt early. Twenty-two children enjoyed an outing to Weston-Super-Mare on 26th June 1939. Shortly afterwards the school received notice from the Education Office that sixty-five children, accompanied by teachers, would arrive from Stoke Church of England School, Coventry.

In the first week of September another group of thirty nine were scheduled to arrive and 'might comprise crippled and blind mothers and children'.

On 3rd September, the day war was declared between Great Britain and Germany, twenty-nine children and five teachers arrived in good spirits. Mr Twigger and the other teachers got together to decide how the school would run when it reopened on the 11th September. When school reopened after six weeks holidays there were twenty new admissions and also thirty-two evacuees from Coventry. This was a total of one hundred and twenty-four children. Mrs Rotherham's offer of a room in her house, 'The Poplars', for a class was gratefully accepted. Miss Clutterluck, from Coventry, taught twelve senior girls there. Mr Ash, His Majesty's Inspector, visited to see how the emergency system was working.

One of the evacuees from Coventry, Beryl Laws, in an interview with the BBC for 'WWII People's War', remembers her family's evacuation to Barford:

***We had a lovely modern house in Coventry, however when we were evacuated to Barford, things changed. We, mothers and children, were taken on a school bus and because my father had a car he was able to follow behind. We were dropped off at the village hall and Barford residents came out to meet us. We were adopted by a couple, with no children, who lived in a quaint thatched roofed cottage. We had to get our drinking water from a pump in the garden, and the bath was filled up with warm water that had been heated in a kettle.***

***In spite of all this we had a great time and were happily scared to death by a neighbour who, after the death of her husband or son in the War had gone a little crazy. Shortly after our evacuation a bomb destroyed our house. We stayed in Barford, moving to what was called a bothy, and then to a house. We had to climb a hill to get pails of water from the big house. We had lots of room, enjoyed the farm and the land girls and watched Italian prisoners being marched up the hill to the prisoner of war camp at the Asps. We also waved and smiled at our English troops as they marched by. Barford turned out to be a very good spot for us.***

Joyce Perrott was eight when the War started and remembers the evacuees attending the school, including one who became a great actress:

***The War started when I was eight and I can remember going home to lunch and my parents listening to the one o'clock news on the wireless, not quite realising the seriousness of it. Initially, we had evacuees from Coventry, among them Billie Whitelaw and later more evacuees from Islington, London. People who had large enough rooms were forced to take them and there was a certain amount of dismay when it was discovered that their mothers came too. One day, when my father went to his allotment, to his surprise he saw two young evacuees running away in fright, green apples falling from their knicker legs as they went! Most of the evacuees found it difficult to settle in such a different environment and returned home.***

***Winning the War became an important issue to us all and I certainly felt personally responsible at a young age. We would collect tins, jars, bottles and newspapers for the war effort and iron railings were removed to be recycled. There were 'Warship weeks', 'Battle of Britain' weeks and 'Dig for Britain' weeks, where concerted efforts were made by everyone in the village to do their bit.***

Kathleen Davis recalls the bathing arrangements set up for the evacuees:

***And we had evacuees come to live in all those little cottages down on the main street at Barford, from the church down past the school there were a lot of little cottages with no bathrooms. Didn't have such things in those days. So the people in charge of the evacuees used to bring them up to the Red House twice a week for the children to have baths, and what a mess they made! We had three bathrooms at the Red House, one with a great big bath. I think they probably put all the kids in together, wouldn't surprise me.***

The Church Lamp, the parish magazine, published a request in 1939 asking that those who had care of the evacuees should help take care of their religious education.

Infants were to attend Sunday School at 10.15 am and the elder ones were to attend church at 2.30 pm. Also the children were to be informed that it was not the custom in Barford to use the swings in the playing fields on Sundays.

A further two evacuees arrived on the 27th September. All pupils left the school in thirty seconds during an evacuation practice in late September.

Mrs Oldham gave a demonstration of home canning of fruit at her home, Forge Cottage, to the senior children.

Mr Twigger was a keen gardener; in fact some of his past pupils say they learned more about gardening than other subjects from him!

He obtained Local Education Authority approval for taking additional land for the school garden. Anthony (Tony) Tallis was one of the senior boys sent, in class time, to work on the allotments. Mr Twigger would visit later on his bicycle. Tony thinks that the Headmaster sold the produce to the parents.

Money for gas mask containers, £1. 15s. 7d. was collected from the children in late November 1939. Tony Tallis was a bit scared by some of the demonstrations in the use of gas masks:

***I attended Barford Church of England School where we had gas mask drill in the mornings. Teacher held her hand underneath the cylinder to cut off the air supply to check for air tightness – we gasped for air!***

***Many people stopped carrying gas masks after years of no gas attacks. When I went to Barford School without mine Mr Twigger, the Head, sent me home for it!***

Joyce Perrott was not impressed with the gas mask drill either:

***We were issued with gas masks and officials visited us at school to make sure they fitted properly. Imagine the pandemonium with a class of thirty-two children trying to inhale deeply enough so that a piece of paper would stick on the end and then exhaling, producing rude noises all round!***

In May 1940 all the children were, again, ordered to carry gas masks following the invasion of Holland and Belgium by Germany. By October this threat was still there and work commenced on the erection of an air raid shelter at the entrance to the boys' play area.

It had been decided that should an air raid warning be sounded while children were at school, the children would be dismissed immediately. The great majority would be sent home, which would entail a journey of not more than eight minutes. Those who could not reach their homes in that time could be taken into friends' houses near to the school. The remaining few could be accommodated in the Rectory cellar.

The school managers had 'darkened' the middle classroom and the infants' room in order that there might be a place where parochial activities could be carried on during the winter evenings: Brownies on Monday, Scouts on Tuesday, library on Wednesday, choir practice on Thursday and Sunday afternoon was used to give an opportunity for evacuated children to meet their parents.

Tony Tallis and his school friends soon became expert at aircraft recognition, both British and German as Tony recalls:
***The German aircraft had a strange throbbing drone noise to their engines. That was the most reliable way to tell the difference. The speeds were so slow we had plenty of time to watch the bombers. One morning, before school, we saw Dakota planes towing Horsa Gliders over Barford village. The aircraft had black and white stripes on the wings. We knew then that 'D-Day' had arrived.***

Joyce Perrott remembers:

***When I was six and my sister Beryl was seven we caught diphtheria, as did two teenage girls, one of whom helped our mother in the house. I learned years later that their brother, who was in the navy at Portsmouth, had brought the infection to the village but fortunately this time it spread no further. We were taken to the local fever hospital, Heathcote, now the rehabilitation hospital, and were not allowed visitors for the whole time we were there. This was a traumatic experience for small children and several young patients died while we were there. Our GP, Dr George Tibbets, diagnosed the disease by its distinctive odour as soon as he came into the bedroom. We had to have complete bed rest and when we returned home we were pale and could hardly walk, but we had survived!***

In the summer of 1940 the school organised a collection of metal, bones and rags for the Warwick Rural District Salvage Scheme. The children also brought clothes into school for distribution among the homeless children of Coventry.

Boys over the age of twelve were permitted to work in school hours to help with the harvest. Mr Twigger was very enthusiastic and had the children out working on the allotments and helping on the farms whenever they could. He met with local farmers to discuss the arrangements for the harvest. In September the school was closed for the Summer months, the children were sent out to pick fruit, including elderberries, rosehips and damsons for the WI jam making project. In September 1941, 119lb of elderberries were picked for the WI.

In 1941, the school children performed a 'delightful entertainment' in the Memorial Hall. The Leamington Courier reported:

***The organisation was in the capable hands of Mr A S Twigger. The infants, trained by Mrs Sarsfield, played singing games. The juniors performed a Nativity play and the seniors a sketch, 'Ghosts'. Gerald Mason won an intelligence test for seniors. Mrs Barker, Mrs H Price and Miss Witherington undertook the difficult task of judging the fancy dress competition.***

***Prizes were awarded to the following infants, D Udell (Dig for Victory), S Udell (Oxo), R Pitcher (Salvage), R Hirons (Peace and War), D Collett (Fairy), M Killian (Painter), D Hemmings (Uncle Sam), A Harding (Nurse), J Rouse (Rat), V Cheshire (National Savings), J Bayliss (Patchwork), J Partridge (Salvage man), Peter Reed (Dutch boy), E Green (Oxo), C Chapman (Turkey), J Hicken (Blackout), Pat Reed (Restless night).***

***The musical parcel was won by D Udell and the spot dance by L Isaacs and B Law. The youngest child in the room, baby Reed, aged 4 months, also won a prize. Everyone was pleased that the Rector had recovered from his accident and he spoke a few words. Mrs Beckingham was at the door. The proceeds were in aid of the Red Cross.***

Another treat, away from school, was the school children's party Mrs V A Cartwright held in the Memorial Hall in January 1942. A team of willing helpers prepared a very fine tea and the guests did the splendid food ample justice. Crackers followed tea then the children enjoyed dancing and games. Mr Twigger thanked Mrs Cartwright on behalf of his pupils.

The horror of war was never far from mind in these years, even for the children.

According to Tony Tallis:
***The Memorial Hall showed films and newsreels. I remember the first films of Belsen concentration camp. All children had to leave the hall, as the film was too dreadful for them to watch. My father insisted I stayed and only one girl was allowed to watch with me.***

The Education Act promising 'Equality of opportunity for all' came into operation on the 1st of April 1945. Shortly after this the war in Europe drew to a close and on the 8th May the children enjoyed two days' national holiday for Victory in Europe (VE). However it was not until the war against Japan ended on the 2nd of September 1945 that the announcement came that 'The world is now at peace'.

The school closed on the 14th September to allow the children to go on an excursion to Barry Island, as a victory celebration. There was further cause for celebration when the school was again closed on the 22nd October on the occasion of a visit to Warwick by Field Marshall Mongomery.

## Seaford Ladies College, Sussex, and other visitors, at Westham House

For the duration of the War Seaford Ladies College, from Sussex, was based at Westham House. The principal, Miss Witherington, joined the WI and encouraged the girls to get involved in village organisations. In December 1940 the Seaford Ladies put on a Nativity tableau in the Memorial Hall for the local children. In December 1941 the girls sang carols at the Women's Institute Christmas meeting.

Janice Scowling was an evacuee at Westham and recalls:

***I was four at the start of the War when our school was evacuated to a manor house at Barford, Warwickshire. The first term was eighteen weeks long with no visits from parents. I was the youngest pupil by two years. Catching the train at Paddington each term was awful, I did not wash the spot of my mother's last kiss for some time. At school the little ones were protected from the news though the older ones heard the nine o'clock news. We saw the planes in the sky for the raids on Coventry and the thousands of planes going over in the early morning on 'D-Day'.***

***Breakfast was lumpy porridge, bread and margarine or jam, never both. On Sundays we had stewed fruit and pastry squares and custard. I cannot stand macaroni cheese and pilchards to this day! However Sharpe's toffees were a great treat, twice a week.***

***We all caught every conceivable childhood disease in spite of being given cod liver oil, malt and syrup of figs every Sunday.***

***We had clean clothes once a week. These included, in winter woollen vests, liberty bodices, woolen stockings with suspenders, long navy knickers and viyella shirts. We had a very sheltered war but it left me with a resolve never to send my children away to school.***

Frances Harvey and Mary Winnington remember the girls school at Westham House:

***Seaford Ladies College evacuated to Westham House during the War. The girls would borrow Maud Workman's bike, which she left propped up against the wall. They would leave a note and later Maud would find it returned to the exact same place. Westham House at the time of writing is an adult college, but in the war it was used for a ladies college. The children came from Seaford in Sussex with their teachers. Some children from the village went there.***

Joyce Perrott had a competitive spirit that was rewarded:

***I remember, as part of National Savings Week, we were invited to design a poster. My effort won the first prize of a fifteen shilling savings certificate. My greatest delight was beating the 'posh' girls of Seaford Ladies College!***

A S Twigger writes of a 'mutually pleasant interlude, particularly in the years of hardship' that resulted from the arrival of Seaford Ladies College. 'Both staff and pupils entered into every phase of village life making their ultimate departure quite sad.'

Miss Witherington was delighted to learn that Westham House was to become a residential college on the departure of the Seaford Ladies College. She said in an interview with the Stratford Herald:

***On returning to the school's old home by the sea the staff and girls will take happy memories of their stay in Warwickshire. The people of Barford have been so very kind to us. We have enjoyed the opportunity for farming on a small scale and Westham House is ideally suited as a centre where all kinds of people may be trained in the importance of agriculture in the life of a healthy nation. As a parting gesture of good will to Barford the girls will present another Nativity play at Christmas.***

In St Peter's Church Vestry meeting minutes there is a note made on the 17th January 1946 of the departure from Barford of the Seaford Ladies College and acknowledging their splendid service to the church for the past five years. The College presented a silver paten to the church.

In August 1943 Westham House was the venue for the 6th annual summer school of the Baha'i Faith. The Leamington Courier describes The Baha'i Faith as:

***A world religion founded by Baha'u'llah (1817 – 1892), who lived in Persia and Iraq and died in Palestine.***

Forty-nine people from all parts of England, two Americans and two Persians came to Westham House and were given lectures on various aspects of the faith. Baha'i ***'Work peacefully to achieve spiritual and practical unity for the whole human family.'***

## Barford Hill House

Sonia Farley (née Hirons) lived at Barford Hill House during the War years. Her father was a stud groom and her mother worked in the linen room. She was a very fine needlewoman. She was later promoted to cook. Sonia remembers some of the eighty-six rooms of the house roped off for the Czech and Polish armies and then for the land girls. American soldiers used to come to meet the land girls there.

Sonia remembers: ***It was a child's paradise. In wartime they took the tennis courts down and they had two pens built there where they used to milk the cows. During the war years the young people went everywhere with Charles Smith-Ryland and the family in an open-top Bentley, stopping at hotels for meals. Princess Margaret used to visit. You could be as scruffy as you liked and Charles didn't care. There was a party nearly every Saturday night, in the winter, when the hunting had finished. There was a darts room, a domino room and a card room. We used to get up to some real antics! In summer there were picnics on the cricket field and there used to be an old wooden railway round the field.***

# THE FALLEN

REMEMBERING THE FALLEN

## S/154714 Private John Finch
## Royal Army Service Corps

John J Finch was born in Warwick in 1917 to John Henry and Rose Finch (née Watts). The family had previously lived in Meriden and Tamworth where John's two brothers, William and Eric, and sister, Rosemary, were born. The Finches moved to The Asps, Barford, and John attended Barford School.
Eric emigrated to Canada in 1931. By 1941 the family were living in Oxfordshire.

John joined the Royal Army Service Corps and saw action in Egypt but was killed in action while tending a wounded comrade on 6th December 1941, aged 24.

He is buried in the Halfaya Sollum War Cemetery, Egypt.

He is commemorated on the Barford Memorial Screen and the Bishop's Tachbrook War Memorial.

## Midshipman (A) Lawrence Edward Willoughby Byam
## HMS Daedalus, Royal Naval Volunteer Reserve

Lawrence was born in 1922, the son of Lieutenant Colonel William Byam, Royal

Army Medical Corps, and Doris Mabel Byam of Marylebone, London. Dr Byam was a distinguished Harley Street doctor. The Duke of York, soon to become King George VI, was included amongst his patients.

The family moved to Barford in 1940 and lived in the Old Mill House after being bombed out of their London house. Lawrence went to preparatory school where he learnt to box and then to Harrow School where he was an excellent sportsman and once played cricket at Lords.

He went up to Oxford for a short time but was invited by Fleet Air Arm to train in Trinidad as an observer/navigator on a Swordfish aircraft. He took part in the Battle of the Atlantic, searching for and destroying German U-boats with rockets and flying from converted oil and grain carriers which were known as Merchant Aircraft Carriers.

On 30th July 1941 the family were informed that Lawrence had been missing since 29th July when his plane failed to return from a flight. Subsequently, on 11th February 1942, a formal presumption of his death was made. He was aged 19 at his death.

He is commemorated on the Lee-on-Solent Memorial, Hampshire, the Barford Memorial Screen and also Harrow School Roll of Honour.

## 75748 Major Maurice Barker
## 12th Prince of Wales, Royal Lancers RAC

Maurice was born on August 16th 1916, to Kenward Stuart Barker and Mary Mabel Barker, née Cooper, of Watchbury House, Barford. The Barkers were married in 1903 and bought the Watchbury estate in 1904.

He was the youngest son, having an older brother, Gordon, and two sisters, Kathleen and Violet. Gordon was a colonel in the Royal Dragoon Guards and was awarded a DSO in 1945.

Maurice attended Stowe School and Trinity College, Cambridge, gaining a BA in 1938.

He enlisted with the 12th Prince of Wales' Lancers and was rapidly promoted to Major.

He died on Wednesday 5th November aged 25, at sea, on his way to the Middle East whilst serving in the 2nd Armoured Brigade, 1st Armoured Division.

He is buried in Stellawood Cemetery, Durban, Kwazulu-Natal, South Africa.

He is also commemorated on the Barford Memorial Screen and Trinity College Chapel Memorial.

## 41136 Lieutenant the Honourable Gustavus Lascelles Hamilton-Russell

Gustavus Hamilton-Russell was born 18th October 1907 in London to Gustavus William Hamilton Russell, 9th Viscount Boyne, and Lady Margaret Selina Lascelles.

He was educated at Eton and Magdalen College, Cambridge, graduating with a BA. He married Joan Verena Lloyd-Verney on 20th January 1931. They had two children, Gustavus Michael in 1931 and Charmian Joan in 1933. Charmian Joan died tragically in Lord Bearsted's house in London while her parents were at the Cornonation Service in Westminster Abbey of George V1 in May 1937. Lord Bearsted also owned Upton House, near Banbury. Mrs Joan Hamilton-Russell died suddenly in April 1938. The family lived in Westham House in Barford from 1936 – 1940.

Gustavus joined the Foot Guards on the 18th January 1929 and gained the rank of lieutenant in the Grenadier Guards. He served in France and Belgium and died of wounds in Dover on 2nd June 1940, aged 32.

At the time of his death the family were living in Shropshire and he is buried at St Lawrence's Church, Burwarton, Shropshire.

He is commemorated on the Memorial Screen in Barford Church.

## 5192894 Private William Pumfrey
## 70th Battalion, Gloucester Regiment

William was born in 1924 in Tewkesbury to Herbert and Emily Pumfrey (née Price).

He was one of four sons, but the firstborn died aged 3 months, and the youngest died at birth. His surviving brother, Frederick joined the Grenadier Guards and survived the War.

The family moved to Barford and William joined the Gloucesters. Sadly he was killed on 27th April 1942, aged 18, during training at Bath.

He is buried in Barford Cemetery and is commemorated on the Barford Memorial Screen.

## 1260185 Aircraftman Richard Herbert Hadley
## Royal Air Force Volunteer Reserve

Richard was born in 1916 in Barford to John and Edith Hadley (née Hemmings). John Hadley was a butcher. The family lived with George Hadley the village sub-postmaster at the Post Office on Wellesbourne Road.

Richard had two brothers, Edward and Anthony, and three sisters, Joyce, Joan, and Beatrice Olwyn, all born in Barford.

After growing up in Barford, Richard joined the Royal Air Force Volunteer Reserve and was posted out to Ceylon, taking part in the action against the Japanese in the run-up to the Battle of Ceylon, which occurred in April 1942.

Richard was killed in action on 25th March 1942, aged 26.

He is buried in Colombo Kanatte General Cemetery and is commemorated on the Barford Memorial Screen.

## D/JX 146785 Able Seaman Harry Conlon
## Royal Navy HMS Diamond

Harry Conlon was born in Birmingham in 1920, the son of John and Ethel Conlon. His father died when he was a very small child. Harry came with his mother to live in Mill Lane, Barford, when his mother married Charles Beck. Charles and Ethel had a son, born in 1928, Ernest Beck, who died in 1947.

Harry joined the Royal Navy when he was sixteen years old. He learnt to box and also enjoyed playing hockey while in service.

He was on board the HMS Diamond and witnessed as the destroyer rescued survivors from the troopship Slamat in the Mediterranean on the 27th April 1941. Many of these survivors had been machine-gunned and torn to shreds in the water. During the passage of the HMS Diamond to Souda Bay in Crete the destroyer came under attack and was sunk, south of Morea. There were only eighteen survivors.

Harry was killed when he was aged 21.

He is commemorated on the Plymouth Naval Memorial and the Barford War Memorial.

## P/MX85530 Alfred Aubrey Upstone
## HMS Polyanthus, Royal Navy

Aubrey was born in 1923, to Francis and Daisy Upstone, née White, of Upton, Worcestershire. The family lived in various parts of the county and settled at Gooseberry Hall Farm in Hareway Lane, Barford.

Daisy died in 1945 in Warwick aged 54 and Francis aged 90 in Stratford upon Avon in 1974.

Aubrey joined the Royal Navy and served as a sick berth attendant on HMS Polyanthus, a Flower-class corvette.

Whilst on escort with two other ships for convoy ON 202 she was struck by an acoustic torpedo fired by U-boat 952 and Aubrey was lost at sea on 20th September 1943, aged 20.

He is commemorated on the Portsmouth Naval Memorial, Hampshire.

He is also commemorated on the Barford Memorial Screen.

## Squadron Leader Henry Eric Maudslay
## Royal Air Force, 617 Squadron

Henry was born in 1921 in Leamington Spa to Reginald and Susan Maudslay. His sister Kate was eleven years older than him. His father was the founder of the Standard Motor Company and another family member was the managing director of the Maudslay Motor Company at Coventry.

In 1925 the family moved to Sherbourne Priors, Watery Lane now a language school. His father died when Henry was only thirteen years old. Henry attended Eton from 1935 until 1940. He was an excellent athlete, as a long distance runner and oarsman. Henry's family moved from Sherbourne to Worcestershire in 1935. Reginald and Susan Maudslay are buried in Sherbourne Churchyard.

Henry was called-up in July 1940 and in September that year he was accepted for pilot training. In November he single-handedly attacked two enemy cargo vessels, which resulted in Maudslay being awarded the Distinguished Flying Cross. In 1943 he was promoted to squadron leader and became B Flight Commander of the new 617 Squadron being formed.

He was a pilot of one of the nineteen aircraft which left Scampton on the 16th May in timed waves, ten minutes apart, to allow them to be directed to the German dams not breached. Eight planes did not return. On his way back from bombing the Eder Dam, Maudslay's plane was shot down close to the Dutch border, with the loss of all the crew.

This operation was the Dam Busters Raid and gave a real boost to civilian and service personnel in the dark days of 1943.

It is estimated that thirteen hundred people died on the ground during this raid, half of them Allied prisoners of war.

Henry Maudslay is buried in the Reichswald Forest War Cemetery.

He is commemorated on a plaque in Sherbourne Church and at the Dam Busters Memorial at Woodhall Spa in Lincolnshire.

# SOME OF THE MEN WHO RETURNED FROM ARMED SERVICE

## George Worrall
## Warwickshire Yeomanry

Like his father Ernest before him, George was a skilled blacksmith. The family forge was in High Street, Barford.

George enlisted in the Warwickshire Yeomanry in 1939. In 1940 the force was sent to Palestine on a peacekeeping mission. It was the only cavalry force in operation during WWII and was attached to the 1st Cavalry Division, 6th Cavalry Brigade. It was also the last cavalry force to see active service.

George's skills as a blacksmith were essential. Cavalry, rather than Infantry, were chosen as the mode of transport for this peacekeeping force as the terrain was difficult, sandy and hilly.

As well as a peacekeeping role, the force was to guarantee the safe flow of much needed oil supplies from the region. More men and horses soon followed bringing the force up to about three thousand men.

The regiment disembarked at Haifa on 9th January 1940 and set up camp at Afula. Against veterinary advice, the horses were not exercised during the voyage from England. The Warwickshire Regiment was the only one who did not suffer any loss of their horses. At Haifa the horses were loaded onto open rail trucks and had great difficulty keeping their footing because of slippery wooden floors.

It is likely that George would have been kept very busy tending to such a large number of horses in the heat, with swarms of flies and at times heavy rain.

In fact conditions were so bad for the men attending the horses that they were excused guard and similar duties for a week after disembarkation.

George must have missed home very much in such an unfamiliar and challenging environment.

According to a Barford village resident, some of the horses came from Barford Hill and as the Barford men knew their temperament they were rather cautious in dealing with them.

Saddles were not introduced until the 18th of January and this was also the day the horses met their new regimental conscripts, the camels. At this first introduction, pandemonium reigned, but soon the horses accepted that these strange beasts were part of their new experience.

As the Regiment moved around they had to endure heavy rain and, combined with the heat, this must have been very uncomfortable. The land around them was still ploughed by wooden implements, pulled by a variety of animals. At one camp they were surrounded by well-maintained and irrigated citrus groves.

At times the commanders, accompanied by some men, went to visit the local village elders and it was considered rude to refuse the gift of a tasty morsel, a sheep's eye! It was also considered bad manners not to burp after a meal!

Christmas 1940 would have been sad for the Warwickshire men in the desert as news reached them of the bombing of Coventry and Birmingham.

In March 1941 the Regiment became mechanised and handed over some of their horses to the Staffordshire and Cheshire Yeomanry.

After this most of the regiment moved to Nablus except for the farriers, probably including George, who went to those other regiments of the brigade who were still cavalry. By April 1941 nearly all the horses were gone, replaced by trucks and tanks, so the men who were farriers had to become engineers.

The 8th Army, of which the Warwickshire Yeomanry was part, first went into action as part of the Allied operation to relieve the besieged city of Tobruk in November 1941.

The Regiment fought at the Second Battle of El Alamein, attached to the 2nd New Zealand Division. The Second Battle of El Alamein took place over twenty days in November 1942 and the Allies' victory here marked a major turning point in the Western Desert Campaign. Lieutenant General Bernard Montgomery commanded the Regiment.

The Warwickshire Yeomanry records indicate that George Worrall fought in this battle.

An eyewitness account of the fighting stated that:

***The German and Italian anti-tank guns opened fire upon the charging tanks silhouetted by the rising sun. German tanks, which had penetrated between the Warwickshire Yeomanry and Royal Wiltshire Yeomanry, also caused many casualties. The more we advanced the more we realised that the Italians did not have much fight in them and after putting up a strong resistance to our overwhelming advance they started surrendering to our lead troops in droves. There was not much action to see but we came across lots of burnt out Italian tanks that had been destroyed by our tanks. I had never seen a battlefield before and the sight of so many dead was sickening.***

The Allied casualties of thirteen thousand five hundred were small in comparison to the Axis casualties of thirty-seven thousand.

Winston Churchill famously summed up the battle of November 1942 with the words, “This is not the end; it is not even the beginning of the end. But it is, perhaps, the end of the beginning.”

It was Montgomery’s greatest triumph and he was ably assisted by our Warwickshire men.

Following the 8th Army victory at the Second Battle of El Alamein they were involved in the Italian Campaign, including the invasion of Sicily. They remained in combat in Italy until 1945. At the end of the war, George was offered a position with the Palestinian Police Force but decided to return to Barford.

Kathleen Davis recalls George’s return home:
***George Worrall came home from the 8th Army with his bride. My cousin was in the 8th Army as well, with the tanks, probably the same lot as George. My cousin died young, probably the shock of it all.***

The minutes of St Peter’s Church Vestry meeting record that, on 10th March 1942, Mr E L Watson and Mr G Worrall, who are serving with H M Forces, were co-opted onto the Church Council in their absence.

**George Worrall**

## Edmund Gilbert Higgitt
## Worcestershire Regiment

Edmund was born on 24th January 1909, the son of Gilbert and Charlotte Higgitt. Gilbert was a sadler and harnessmaker and had his home and business premises in Church Street, Barford. Edmund was baptised in St Peter's Church Barford on 28th March 1909. He joined the Worcestershire Regiment and was taken prisoner of war in Tobruk in 1942. From Tobruk Edmund was transported in the hull of a ship and taken to Italy. Once there the prisoners were forced to march to a camp, through towns where people shouted, laughed and even spat at them. Once in the camp food was scarce, just bread and water, and bed was a hole in the sand. Every man was covered in fleas. After a long time they were moved by train and cattle trucks.

Edmund was released in 1945. He returned to live with his brother in the family home in Barford. David Hemmings remembers Eddie (Edmund) living with his brother Walter, a mechanic, in one of the cottages on Bridge Street. He enjoyed a breakfast of beer and pickled onions. Edmund seems not to have recovered from his wartime experience, and was not the outgoing man who enlisted.

Edmund died in 1984.

## Private A Huckvale

Private Huckvale, prisoner of war, also returned home in 1945. The Huckvale family had lived in Barford since the middle of the 18th century. Two older brothers of Private Huckvale were killed in WWI.

## Joseph Albert Thomas Freeman

Joseph, who lived in Mill Lane was called up in August 1944. He served with the Worcester and Herefordshire Regiment in Germany, taking part in the crossing of the River Elbe and the River Weser. Joseph Freeman's brother, William, served on a minesweeper with the Royal Navy. Both brothers attended Barford School.

## Private Charles Pitcher

Charles Pitcher of Sandy Way was wounded whilst serving with the Parachute Regiment, crossing the River Rhine. He also attended Barford School.

## Major Oswald Tritton
## Royal Field Artillery WWI/Observer Corps WWII

Major Oswald Tritton was born in 1875 in London. He was a first cousin of Lord Willoughby de Broke. He married Violet Margaret Sedgwick in August 1914. He came to Barford in 1920. He lived in Rose Cottage, Wellesbourne Road, and then at Capers, Wellesbourne Road, Barford until he died in March 1963. He was very involved in the British Legion, both in Barford and in Warwickshire, and was also involved with the Home Guard during WWII.

Major Tritton unveiled the Barford War Memorial.

## Lieutenant Colonel Ernest Leonard Watson
## Royal Army Ordnance Corps

Ernest Leonard Watson was born in Hendon, Middlesex. His grandfather, John A Watson OBE, was a former high sheriff of Warwickshire. Ernest was an engineer. He came to live in Woodlands, Hareway Lane, just after it was built, in the 1920s, with his wife Hilda and their family. He was commissioned into the army as a second lieutenant. He was given a Regular Army Emergency Commission and promoted to temporary major in 1941.

During the 1930s Hilda Watson was very involved with the Girl Guides and presented a photograph of the Chief Scout and Chief Guide to Barford Girl Guides in 1933. Ernest was made County Commissioner of Boy Scouts for Warwickshire in June 1946. He died in March 1983.

# Harry Abbott

Harry Abbott served in WWI and in the Home Guard during WWII. He worked for Mr Smith-Ryland in their timber yard. He later lived at 7 Church Street. His son Harry Abbott joined the Coldstream Guards before WWII, and became a sergeant major. The poster shows him as the best dressed serviceman at that time in WWII. There were two other Abbott brothers in the army, George and Charles.

## Brigadier General Sir Atwell Charles Baylay
## GOC Infantry Brigade/Royal Field Artillery

Brigadier Baylay lived in Barford House from 1938 until the 1950s. He was born in 1879, the son of Colonel F G Baylay. He was commissioned in the Royal Engineers in 1898. In 1912 he took up the appointment with the Royal Monmouthshire Royal Engineers, which he held until 1915. He then became OC 1st (West Riding) Field Company RE, attached to 29th Division. He commanded his unit until December 1916, both on Gallipoli and the Somme. He retired with the honorary rank of Brigadier General in 1919. In 1936, just before he came to live in Barford, he was Chairman of the Birmingham and District Engineering Employers Association. His wife was the daughter of Governor J B Groome of Maryland, USA. They had one daughter. In 1947 he was knighted but shortly after this his wife Maria died.

Brigadier Baylay took the salute at the Armistice Day Parades in Barford during his time living in the village. He died on the 6th October 1957.

## Lieutenant John Watson
## Royal Warwickshire Regiment

Lieutenant Watson lived in Mill Lane, Barford, for a number of years. He served in WWI with distinction. During WWII he was a reserve officer and was promoted from lieutenant to second lieutenant. He was reported missing shortly after 18th April 1941. It is likely that he was part of the British Infantry Brigade that was part of the British Commonwealth contingent of thirty-nine thousand, which was sent to help protect Crete from the Italian and German armies. On April 25th 1941 Hitler had ordered the invasion of Crete, which was the first truly large-scale airborne invasion of the war. Over twelve thousand British Commonwealth troops, including Lieutenant Watson, were captured.
It was reported in the Leamington Spa Courier in October 1943 that Mrs J Watson, Mill Lane, had received a letter concerning her husband. At this time John Watson had been a prisoner of war for more than two and a half years.

This letter was from a fellow officer who was writing from the SS Drottningholm. He said that he had left Lieutenant Watson only a week previously in Rotenburg Prisoner of War Camp, in Southern Germany. He was very well and in excellent form, well off for bedding and clothing and asks for nothing further in that line to be sent to him. His fellow officer said that John was always cheery, assisting with the heating of water for evening drinks for five hundred officers. The Red Cross parcel supply to Rotenburg was good and the attitude of the Germans had improved. Lieutenant Watson returned home to Barford in April 1945.

## Lieutenant Colonel Cyril H Price
## 32nd Sikh Pioneers 2/12 Frontier Force Regiment

Cyril H Price was born in 1900 to Rev Hugh and Edith Price in 16 Sutton Street, Aston, Birmingham, where Hugh was the vicar of St Mary's Church. Cyril had an older brother, Allen.

On 3rd October 1914, aged 14, Cyril embarked on the ship Mongolia to Bombay.

Cyril joined the army and during WWI he served in India with 32nd Sikh Pioneers where he attained the rank of lieutenant. He came home in 1920 for a while to the Rectory in Barford where his father was now a canon and incumbent at St Peter's.

Cyril continued to serve in India and by 1921. He was a second lieutenant with 34th Pioneers and in 1923 with the 84th Pioneers. On 16th May 1924 he left Bombay for London on the Macedonia, returning to Bombay on the Mantola on 26th June 1926. On 9th October 1928 Captain Price left Liverpool for Bombay on the Britannia. Later, on 17th September 1932, he left the RAC Club at 6 Pall Mall, SW1, for Bombay on the Viceroy.

On the 14th September 1935 he travelled from Liverpool to Bombay on Britannia. At the outbreak of WWII he was asked to reform a Sikh regiment that had been disbanded in 1932.

Quote from the History of the Sikh Regiments:

***The excellence of the Mazhabi and Ramdasias as soldiers in the old Sikh Pioneer regiments from 1857 to their disbandment in 1932 was well known to our fine commander in chief, Colonel C H Price and our fine second-in-command, Major E P F Pearse. They had experienced the joy and pride of serving with the Mazhabi and Ramdasias in the old Pioneer Regiments. They had experienced the sorrow of the disbandment in 1932. In 1942 these two officers were presented with the opportunity to help the Mazhabi and Ramdasias regain their old position in the Indian Army.***

***The enthusiasm of these two officers was revered by all who served with them and was an important element in the growth of the new regiment, which was raised at Jullundur.***

The 1st Mazhabi and Ramdasias fought in Burma and were later named 1st Sikh Light Infantry.

A newspaper article in the Leamington Courier on the 8th March 1946 reads:

***Lieutenant Colonel C H Price, second son of Canon and Mrs Hugh Price of Barford, has been presented with a Japanese sword by all ranks of 1st Battalion Sikh Light Infantry which has just returned from Burma and which was created through his efforts.***

In 1948 he married Agnes Cox and he died on 4th March 1963 in Warminster.

# Captain Frank Owen

Captain Owen was a survivor of the notorious Japanese prisoner of war camps. He was captured at the fall of Singapore and was incarcerated at Changi Jail before being transported to Thailand to work as a slave labourer on the infamous Burma-Siam 'Death Railway'.

More than twelve thousand Allied prisoners along with at least ninety thousand Asian labourers perished during the construction of the two hundred and fifty-eight-mile railway line between Bangkok (in Thailand) and Rangoon (in Burma) during 1943. Conditions were singularly horrific; torture, malnutrition, illness and execution were daily perils.

## Westham House College

### APPOINTMENT OF THE FIRST WARDEN

CAPTAIN FRANK E G OWEN, B A., who has been appointed the first Warden of Westham House Adult Residential College and Town and Country Centre at Barford, is a Londoner and 37 years of age

From University College, London, he took his B A Degree (hons in modern history) in 1931, and was a postgraduate at the Department of Business Administration at London School of Economics, and at the National Institute of Industrial Psychology From 1932-33 he was a factory executive in a leading firm of furniture producers, and was despatch manager when called up as a T A gunner officer in August, 1939 In 1941 he was promoted Battery Captain in a 25-pounder field regiment, and no promotion followed as he became a prisoner of war in Japanese hands at Singapore Most of his time was spent as officer-in-charge of non-medical work in a large prisoner hospital, and it was his job to keep the Japs off his men, and secondly to work physically harder than they to show what could be done on rice, the diet to keep the hospital functioning

On 6th August 1945 the USA dropped an atomic bomb on the city of Hiroshima.

Three days later a second device was exploded, destroying Nagasaki. This was followed by the Japanese surrender on 14th August.

With Frank during this horrendous experience were two exceptional artists: Ronald Searle, who made secret drawings of the guards in the style which later became famous in his St Trinian's schoolgirls; and Jack Bridger Chalker ARCA, RWA, Hon SMAA, a professional artist, who, at great personal risk, documented images of the appalling conditions endured by the prisoners.

On returning to England after the War, Frank was advised that he should work in the countryside for the sake of his health. He was appointed as the warden at Westham House which was owned by an educational trust. The house was then an adult education college and provided the peace and quiet of a rural environment to people in need of sanctuary. Jack Chalker agreed to join Frank and instigated highly successful painting courses which ran alongside courses such as Shakespeare and literature studies.

## Major Geoffrey Hobbs

Geoffrey Hobbs, son of a local farmer and wholesale butcher, was a major in the Royal Warwickshire Regiment and served in the Far East. He returned home to Barford before the end of the conflict because he had been badly wounded. After an extended period of convalescence he was demobilised from the forces and was sufficiently recovered to join Oldhams Transport as a manager. He learnt every aspect of the livestock transporting trade from Guy Oldham who had set up Britain's first livestock haulage business in 1928. After a period of nationalisation under the Labour Government followed by diversification into general haulage, Geoffrey eventually became the chairman of the company.

## Norman Gardiner's wartime experience

*The reality of wartime took its course and by the middle of 1941 the conscription age for the armed forces had been lowered to eighteen and a half. Within a couple of days of reaching that age I received notice to report for a medical examination at Coventry. It was a freezing cold frosty morning and I had to catch a bus from Barford at about 6.30 am. There was no heating on at the medical centre and I joined a queue of shivering lads in our underpants in a draughty corridor. In due course my call-up papers arrived telling me to report for duty at Derby on the 14th of May 1942. My Granny Robinson died about a fortnight after I was called-up but I was not granted leave to attend her funeral. I was subsequently called-up to serve with the Royal Army Ordnance Corps. I trained at various locations in the UK before I was posted, in March 1944, initially to Egypt and then to join the 7th Armored Brigade in their thrust through Italy to end up in Austria in May 1945.*

*Life was punctuated with only occasional visits back to Barford on leave. In late 1943, I met my then future wife Jean in Bradford (Yorkshire) and I remember her meeting me in Birmingham as she had travelled down to see Barford for the first time and meet my family. We took the train together to Warwick but as there were no buses running, I managed to cadge a lift on an Oldhams cattle truck to Barford as the driver recognised me. Jean's first view of Barford was from the cab of a smelly truck. She stayed for a long weekend and then we did not meet again for two years, when I returned to England and married her. I was never to return to reside in Barford as, after the war, I made my home in Yorkshire with Jean.*

Norman Gardiner & Jean Driver's marriage 24th December 1945

## Barford flags flying!

The Leamington Courier reported on feelings of thankfulness at the cessation of hostilities on the 24th August 1945. Bright display flags and bunting appeared as if by magic as reported by the Leamington Courier:

***The Rector conducted services at noon and at 6 pm on Sunday large congregations gathered in church to join in the special thanksgiving services. The theme of the Rector's addresses in the morning and evening was 'Fellowship'. A special feature of the evening service was imparted to it by the presence of children with their parents. Major Tritton read the lesson in the morning and in the evening Miss Shirt. We were glad to have Miss Lee back in her place at the organ for the occasion.***

***On Wednesday and Thursday dances were held in the Memorial Hall in aid of the Children's Outing Fund. Mr R Hammond played old time dances on Wednesday and Mr Sim's radiogram supplied the music on Thursday. The helpers were Mr J Simmons, Mrs Gilbert Taylor, Mrs H Tilling, Mrs R Jones, Mrs Inson and Mrs J Simmons. Mr P Hammond gave a basket of apples, Mr R Hammond, flowers, and Mrs W Inson, a dozen eggs as prizes. Miss S Wilson and Mr R Watson won the dance prizes.***

The Parish Council passed a proposal by Warwick District Council to provide thirty houses for men returning from the War. Canon Price retired, due to advancing years, after a memorable rectorship at Barford since 1923. The Rectory, on the same site for hundreds of years, at what is now the Glebe Hotel, was sold by auction on the 6th December 1945; the household effects went to auction of the 11th December 1945. These effects included four suits of chain armour with helmets!

Soon the houses for the returning men would be built. Two large mansions, Barford Hill House and the Red House, were demolished to make way for smaller homes. Other mansions, such as Watchbury, were divided up. The Water Mill, sited on the Avon at the end of Verdon Close for nearly a thousand years, was demolished. The two world wars had changed this small village forever but the spirit of the people – caring, resourceful, creative – remained constant.

Write the address in large BLOCK letters in the panel below.
The address must NOT be typewritten.
TO:-
MISS B O HADLEY
THE LOFT
BARFORD
WARWICK
ENGLAND
481445
Write the message very plainly below this line.
CHRISTMAS GREETINGS FROM
THE MEDITERRANEAN
from Tony
This space should not be used.

## Acknowledgements

This book is a tribute to the soldiers who died, those men who returned, and to the people who lived and worked in Barford during wartime. It was written using personal reminiscences from those who lived here, with help from their families, archives, museums and online resources, for which we are thankful. We have checked all information but despite our best efforts there may be errors. We apologise if there are any mistakes and ask that you let us know so that we can rectify our archives. We have sought permission from all the copyright holders we could identify.

If you would like to learn more, or to contact us, please visit our website: **barfordheritage.org.uk.**

### Museums, archives and websites visited for this book

Imperial War Museum, Leamington Spa Library and Museum, National Archives, Kew, Shakespeare Birthplace Trust Archives, Philip Spinks (War Tribunals), Royal Regiment of Fusiliers Museum, Warwick (thanks to David Baynham), Warwick Record Office (school log books, Rifle Range minute books), Warwickshire Yeomanry Museum, Commonwealth War Graves, De Ruvigny Roll of Honour, Wikipedia, Ancestry, British Library Newspaper Archive, Forces Reunited, Regimental websites.

### Bibliography

Census Records 1891, 1901, 1911, Trade Directories (Kelly's) 1890-1946, Parish Magazine, Leamington Spa Courier, Warwick Advertiser, Stratford Herald, Birmingham Post, Coventry and Warwickshire in the Great War by Chris Holland, Leamington Czech Patriots by Alan Griffin, Fowler's Roll of Honour of the County of Warwickshire, Yeoman: Warwickshire Yeomanry by Paul Baker, BBC, WWI and WWII, recorded interviews.

### Photographs

Barford Heritage Archives, and the following families: Smith-Ryland, Talbot, Conlon (O'Hare), Wardle, Taylor, Barlow, Bradley, Bristow, Worrall, Abbott,

Jordan (Moore), Powers, Byerley, Colson, Cheshire, Schofield, Tallis, A H C Flower, Hemmings, Jones, Gardiner, and Barford WI who very kindly allowed us to copy their photographs. 'Strike Leaders Outbound' (p72-73) image by Philip E. West GAvA - The Art Studio www.aviationfineart.co.uk.

**Special thanks** to Bill Worrall, Jan Bradley, Goff Tilling, Ian Webster, the late Tim Barlow, James Rutter, Derek Powers and the customers of the Scout Hut Cafe for patiently answering our many questions. We would also like to thank the Evetts family for permission to use Hazel Taylor's lovely poem. We appreciate the help of Barford Parish Council. Barford Heritage Group would also like to thank Warwickshire Rural Community Forum for assisting with printing costs.

**Barford Heritage Group 2015**

Editorial Group: Ann McDermott, Wendy Barlow, Carole Whiteley, Maggie Hayward, Hilary Maynard and Doug Warne.

Graphic Design and Contemporary Photography: Carole Whiteley.

Monetary Resources Management: Edward Kirkby, Wendy Barlow.

Research: Ann McDermott, Carole Whiteley, Hilary Maynard, Doug Warne, Wendy Barlow, Maggie Hayward, Elizabeth Harrison-Hall.

Reminiscences Collecting: Wendy Barlow, Maggie Hayward. Reminiscences originally typed by Shirley Osborne in 2010.

Maps Barford 1911: Doug Warne.
Printing Consultants: Elizabeth Harrison-Hall, Ann McDermott, Carole Whiteley.

Proofreading: Nicky Lawrence (née Scott).

Webmaster: Kirsty Healey. Technical assistance: Alan McDermott.

Barford Heritage Group: Elspeth Monks, Sally Hallowell-Carew, Rod Scott, Derek Powers, Gerard Veness, Ken Hope.

We also remember our friend Brenda Barber who in her last week of life recalled the terror of living through the Coventry bombings.

## Index

*Come to the arboretum*
*On a late October day,*
*Where the beauty of the foliage*
*Will take your breath away.*
*Walk with me through winding paths,*
*And peaceful, quiet glades,*
*And share with me the splendour,*
*Of the lovely, autumn shades.*
*The sunlight on the sycamores*
*Turns their leaves to gold,*
*While berries of the holly trees*
*Are ruby red and bold.*
*Study the great cedar tree,*
*It's fine old branches spreading,*
*Which, like the smaller conifers,*
*Ripe cones it is now shedding.*
*Crimson acers glow,*
*Against the pale azure sky,*
*And through the trees,*
*The whispering breezes, softly sigh.*

*Hazel Taylor* *A Barford Villager*